PENGUIN BOOKS

ME AND MY PLAYS

Mahesh Dattani is a playwright, screen writer, film-maker and stage director with several scripts and productions to his credit.

For his writing he was honoured with the prestigious Sahitya Akademi Award in 1998. He has directed and scripted critically acclaimed films like *Mango Soufflé* and *Morning Raga*. The script of *Morning Raga* has been archived by the Academy of Motion Picture Arts and Sciences, USA. His screenplays, along with his stage plays, have been published by Penguin.

Dattani is also a workshop facilitator for several writing and acting courses, having conducted workshops in many parts of the world, most notably at the Portland State University in Oregon, USA. He has collaborated with international theatre companies like Border Crossings, most recently in Shanghai with Chinese, Swedish and English actors. He also writes scripts for BBC Radio 4.

MAHESH DATTANI

Me and My Plays

PENGUIN BOOKS

An imprint of Penguin Random House

PENGUIN BOOKS

USA | Canada | UK | Ireland | Australia
New Zealand | India | South Africa | China

Penguin Books is part of the Penguin Random House group of companies
whose addresses can be found at global.penguinrandomhouse.com

Published by Penguin Random House India Pvt. Ltd
4th Floor, Capital Tower 1, MG Road,
Gurugram 122 002, Haryana, India

Penguin
Random House
India

First published by Penguin Books India 2014

ISBN 9780143422280

Typeset in Sabon by R. Ajith Kumar, New Delhi

Printed at Repro India Limited

www.penguin.co.in

MIX
Paper from
responsible sources
FSC® C047271
www.fsc.org

To Padma and Hansa

Contents

Contents

Me and My Plays

An Essay

Bangalore in the 1960s was considered a pensioner's paradise. It was indeed a paradise of sorts with its salubrious weather, quiet roads and friendly people. There were pockets in the city that housed communities that had migrated from the north of the Vindhyas. We never did fit into the upwardly mobile, wealth-showing community of Gujaratis and we rarely socialized as families. So, it was always an exciting day when we received the community newsletter that occasionally

Facing page: Mahesh Dattani on the sets of *The Big Fat City*. (*Courtesy Salamat Hussain*)

updated us on festival events or deaths and ever so occasionally announced the staging of a Gujarati play at the Town Hall.

My father used to talk very fondly of his days in Bombay (as it was called then, before it was changed to Mumbai in the mid-1990s) when he would visit the theatres at Bhangwadi to see Gujarati musical drama near the city's notorious opium bazaar. He would talk about legends like Motibai, Miss Shyamabai and comedian Chagan 'Romeo', all of whom were stars with a faithful following. Performances would go on for hours longer than scheduled because of the cries of 'once more!' which led to popular song routines being replayed, sometimes almost a dozen times! But all this was just a fairy tale to me. As real as the stories in *Chandamama* that my sister Padma would read out from when I was a child.

I must have been about nine years old when I got to see the real thing. It was at the Town Hall in Bangalore. It seemed so grand in those days with its Roman columns, majestic arches and corridors. I remember the Gujarati community, well turned out in their safari suits and American georgette saris. My mother was probably the most excited of all of us, meeting old friends from her home town. The banter was invariably about weddings, wedding plans and prospective brides and grooms. The men talked only about business and the Africa-returned traders always lorded it over the desis. The shrill bell announcing the start of the play could just about be heard over the loud voices in the foyer, and it did little to cut short the chatter. When even the third bell could not succeed in getting people to move from the foyer into the hall, the local sponsors resorted to desperate pleas imploring people to go inside so that they could start the play.

Inside, the decibel levels did not diminish. In fact, they grew even stronger as people called out to friends across the hall. Class divides were clearly drawn with the local sponsors getting front-row seats, while the rest of us got whatever came to us, scurrying for seats near the fans. The announcements commenced with requests to keep silent and take crying infants out of the auditorium. And then the play began.

After the initial awe of seeing real people on stage, unlike in the movies, I was struck by the loud voices of the actors and their loud costumes. It was a play about well-off Gujaratis. Yes, the women wore georgette and there was a character who had returned from Africa. The woman was meeting her lover secretly at home but the husband returned a little early. There was laughter in the house which died down soon after the husband brought out a gun. I was transfixed by how the mere appearance of the weapon changed the tone of the play entirely. There were sharp intakes of breath as the gun was passed around; the very air crackled with tension. It was clear to all of us—including me with my virgin sense of dramaturgy—that the gun would go off at some point. At one light moment in the play, the gun came to the actress who, turning around to the audience, shot at a man in the front row. Bang!

The man fell off his seat after a loud cry and was rushed out of the hall.

It was only once the house lights came on as the curtain fell that I became aware once again that I was in a hall with a thousand people! There was a palpable silence in the hall before the murmurs picked up again. Only, this time they were talking about the play, especially the twist before the interval. They were keen to know what would happen next. I was fascinated not only by the plot but also the effect the play had on its audience. If something like this could shut the mouths of a thousand Gujaratis, I had to be a part of this magic! This was indeed the beginning of a beautiful relationship.

I came to know much later that the play I had seen was Madhu Rye's acclaimed Gujarati play *Koi Pan Ek Phool Nu Naam Bolo To* (Say the Name of a Flower).

Despite my newfound love for theatre, I had no opportunity to even express my desire to act in a play. It seemed such an impossible dream. But

I recall becoming more attentive to my father's stories of Bhangwadi in the past and the theatres he used to frequent during his business trips to Bombay.

In school I was too shy to try out for the annual school production, usually a Christmas pageant. One year, our class teacher encouraged me to try out for a part. I was cast as one of the angels who visit the manger when Jesus is born. I had no lines but had to flap my arms and throw stardust on the crib. When I got on stage the entire school was watching, including the teachers I was scared of! My knees were shaking and I could barely move my arms! This just didn't seem right. I thanked God (Jesus at that time—because we were told if we didn't believe in him we would go to hell) that I hadn't got a speaking part. I don't think I have ever been as frightened as I was then.

The rest of school was very uneventful. I was average at most subjects although quick at grasping things. This was one of the better (read English-medium) schools in Bangalore. My parents—being in a state that was foreign to them in so many ways—were keen that my sisters and I study in schools that would teach us to speak good English. And English was one of the subjects that I quickly warmed to. It was as though the universe was conspiring to wash my brains of my Gujarati heritage and displace me linguistically. I was fascinated by the English poets, by Dickens and the Lambs' version of Shakespeare because my teachers were so passionate about them. The literature of the state that had adopted me was alien to me. I hadn't even heard of writers like Shivaram Karanth, P. Lankesh, Girish Karnad and, I suspect, neither had my teachers. As for the literatures and language of Gujarat, they were something that my parents indulged in and so were not to be taken seriously. They belonged to the past, and for me, my school and the English language were the present. I didn't realize it at the time, but this attitude would spell my doom in the decades to come.

The actor in me did come out of the closet

on some occasions. I remember a schoolmate, Ramesh, who was as timid as me. Ramesh lived not too far from my home. He had a younger sister and several cousins around our age. I am not sure how interested he was in drama but he played along since it was a source of great amusement to his parents and cousins. I would take a fairy tale like 'Snow White' and get everyone together on Ramesh's terrace. We would rehearse the scenes and also choreograph a little dance. Our costumes were made from bits and pieces of zari and satin that I managed to get from a tailor close by. The clothes line on Ramesh's terrace provided the perfect mechanism on which to drape the curtain (old saris, of course). Our audience comprised Ramesh's parents, uncles and aunts, and many children, all related to him. Those who were not on stage became the audience. At the age of twelve I learnt the benefits of having a large cast in a play. They were sure to bring in their friends and relations as the much-needed audience! This didn't last very long, though, since Ramesh grew bored with the whole thing. It turned out that his interest lay really in cricket. Maybe that is why I still hate the game: it robbed me of a potential collaborator.

By the 1970s I was in college. This may have been a swinging time for the swish set in Bombay or Delhi. But in sleepy Bangalore, it was still a sensational matter if daring girls hitched rides to college or a really bold one clung to the waist of her leather-clad boyfriend riding a Bullet as they zipped down Brigade Road. There was the occasional 'jam session' at a friend's home with some weed being passed around. One heard of worse things but that may have only been the workings of overenthusiastic imaginations and wishful thinking.

In college too, the drama club was appropriated by the lot who were more 'with it'. I did try to get my way in but I guess I was too square for them. The big event was the Spring Festival organized by a rival college. The host college always won the Best Play trophy. Even so, we all looked forward to it—more for the cool Dylan-inspired music and gender mixing than for artistic reasons.

And then came my second significant taste of drama. It happened quite unexpectedly. A friend of a friend was acting in an English play. Tickets were being sold on campus and I decided to check it out. It was a play called *Table Manners* written by an English playwright (Alan Ayckbourn), performed by the Bangalore Little Theatre. This was the first English play that I saw on a public stage. The play was a mild-mannered comedy about people I couldn't really place in my head, unlike the Gujarati whodunnit I had seen as a child. Yet this play was in a language I could understand better—the language I wanted to understand better, the language I spoke in with my friends and my sisters.

There was a different kind of excitement mounting in me. I can only describe it as a close encounter of the third kind. I actually knew one of the actors. This alien but fascinating world was now within my reach. A friend of a friend is only one introduction away! We got ourselves invited to the play's after-party.

The Bangalore Little Theatre or BLT, as it is known still, was in fact looking for volunteers for their future productions. I got a membership form, filled it up and mailed it to the address given on the form. I was now officially a member of a drama company! For an eighteen-year-old in the mid-1970s this was no small achievement.

The BLT newsletters started coming to me and I would read every word and hope there was a casting call. There was! I showed up. I got rejected. This was to become a pattern for some years. Today when I hear of struggling actors being rejected all the time, my heart goes out to them. But I didn't struggle for too long. That is because I gave up. It was clear to me that I wasn't cut out to be an actor. There were two things going against me. My thin, nasally voice and my effeminate gestures. I figured it just wasn't worth the bother to change those. Either I didn't care too much about my acting or I cared too much about myself—I don't know. I just gave it up. Many years later, I became aware of how important training can be to an actor. Acting is not about who you are so much as the possibilities of what you can become. Or maybe I was just too happy being myself and didn't really want to become someone else. I did, however, join some workshops, conducted by a senior member of the group, which changed my perception of acting completely.

Around the late 1970s, a schoolmate named Bimal contacted me. Although Bimal and I were not friends in school, we met because he wanted to share with me his secret passion—theatre! To think we were in the same school, nursing the same interest for theatre. He was very keen to be an actor. He wanted to start a theatre group and wanted me to direct the first play. I had previously done a workshop with BLT for directors, where I had presented a rather well-received short play by George Bernard Shaw called *Passion, Poison and Petrifaction*. Bimal's proposal interested me and I said yes to him. We chose to do Woody Allen's *God*. It was an insane thing to do. The play needed a cast of twenty. Bimal and I were barely out of our teens and he wanted to do a large-scale production for the public. I don't think I knew what I was getting into but I am eternally grateful to Bimal for having the courage to step out of his shell and actually *do* something. He was an inspiration to me. Left to myself, I think I may have been content just dreaming about doing things. He gave me the courage to move on and do far more daring things like writing a play.

By the mid-1980s, I had joined my father in his agency to sell machinery for packaging and printing. At the same time I started my drama group called Playpen. The early productions were all Western plays ranging from a Greek tragedy (done very badly) to Neil Simon. I used to assist my father by visiting our supplier's head office in Bombay. I always timed my visit such that I could catch a play at Prithvi Theatre. On one such trip I happened to see a Hindi play. The audience was completely engrossed in the play, applauding at certain points when hard-hitting lines were delivered with great emphasis. That was a moment of realization for me. It struck me that the culture of the audience and the culture of the characters in the play were the same. They could relate completely with what was happening on stage. The applause and laughter were of recognition. This just didn't happen in my theatre. Maybe I should try something like that, I thought.

I went back home and discovered some Indian plays in English published in a magazine called *Enact*. I read one of them aloud, putting all the feeling I had into the text, but I just couldn't get the same degree of energy and meaning that the Hindi actors could. I then had a reading with friends who wanted to try their hand at acting. They were disappointed it wasn't an English play. I was disappointed the plays in English weren't expressive enough like the Hindi one I had seen. I then saw a Kannada version of *Hamlet*. The play made more sense to its audience in Kannada than if it were performed in the language of the playwright. That's when I realized I was doomed. I didn't have an audience, because I didn't have a language. The kind of text-based theatre I wanted to do could not be possible without a language. I guess my plight was a bit like that of an ambitious runner who suddenly discovers one day that he has no legs. I wanted to speak but I was mute. It is easy today for me to use such analogies to describe what I felt then, but at that time it was all very confusing. There was no synthesis between my feelings, thoughts and actions. All I knew was that I needed to do something.

Out of this necessity came my initial attempts at writing an original play. There was an annual event called the Deccan Herald Theatre Festival, sponsored by a popular paper of the same name. All the English-language theatre groups looked forward to participating in it since it ensured full houses and revenue for the next production. The deadline for submission was round the corner but I had no play. During a lazy afternoon in my dad's office, while my father took his customary nap on a couch, I looked at his sleeping figure for a while and let my imagination run wild. I wrote the beginning of the first scene of my first play—a play about a father and son who couldn't see eye to eye . . . I slipped into a world of fantasy and before my father woke up I had scribbled down a good five pages. I managed to scribble down another five. That evening, when it was time to drive home, I took the portable Remington typewriter with me, which was lying in the office cupboard, unused after we'd bought a fancy Godrej typewriter. If my father was surprised, he didn't ask why.

A few days later I called my actor friends over to my office, which doubled as a reading room and production house after office hours. They were all too keen to know the play I had chosen for the festival. I told them I had a dozen pages of a play that I may want to write at some time—would they be kind enough to read it? They obliged.

I remember that they couldn't stop laughing. I had known I was writing a funny play but I hadn't realized they would find it *that* funny. They unanimously decided that we should do that play for the upcoming theatre festival. The only problem was that I had only about a dozen pages. I also had no idea how I would end it. Moreover, I had three weeks to figure out all this and come up with a typewritten script for the actors to rehearse with. The next day I went over to the *Deccan Herald* office and gave in my details. The title of the play was *Where There's a Will*. I looked at the column that said 'name of the author'. The other groups had put in names like Ingmar Bergman, Harold Pinter and Bertolt Brecht in their forms. Without any hesitation I filled in the column with my name in capitals.

The play was received with laughter, laughter and laughter. The laughter of identification that I had craved for. I was elated when people came backstage in huge numbers congratulating me for writing something they could identify with. They were all too tired of the fake accents on stage and the posturing that went on in the name of theatre in English. It looked like I had unwittingly pointed out that the Emperor had no clothes. Now even the audiences began to openly acknowledge their dissatisfaction with theatre that did not speak to them. To me there was no looking back. Years later when I did *The Tempest* with English director Michael Walling, Caliban's line—'You taught me language; and my profit on't / Is, I know how to curse'—found a resonance with me. I had indeed discovered the language called 'Indian English' and I was ready now to make my indictments on my society.

I don't think I was fully aware that speaking in English had a snob value attached to it. Maybe it was the kind of English I spoke that did not in any way exalt me in the eyes of those who aspired to speak English. This struck me when a reputed actor, known for her superb command of English—which she spoke with the Queen's cadences—told me that I would be better off doing my plays in the market square. I was just as ignorant as she was about street theatre and its impact, so I took umbrage but could not really say much to her because of her seniority.

It was very surprising to me that critics did

not laud my attempt at original writing, hitherto unheard of in English-language theatre in India. (Later, of course, I came to know of well-known Indian English playwrights like T.P. Kailasam, Asif Currimbhoy, Gieve Patel and Partap Sharma.) But then I have discovered that most critics are slaves to their limited concept of theatre and are very unwilling to acknowledge their limitations.

There was also the challenge of finding funds to produce plays. Again, the sponsors fell into the same trap as the critics. They were unwilling to see new trends emerging, and continued to support clumsy productions of *The Sound of Music*. (I concede that there was enormous singing talent in Bangalore, especially among the Christian community, but musical theatre as a specialized art form was beyond our understanding in English-speaking Bangalore circles—be it Indian traditional forms or even the Broadway musicals of the West whose film versions caught the fancy of every choir master and music director in the city.)

I consider myself extremely fortunate that I

found a sponsor in my father. He could see how passionate I was about doing theatre. I remember he had earlier loaned me Rs 4000 for a production that never took off. Decades later, a running joke between us was that I owed him Rs 4000 because I never did do the play I had wanted to do. I told him I would never return that sum because I wanted the debt to spill over into the next life. Indeed it has. That sum is now a token of my debt of gratitude to my parents, which can never be repaid.

I had another passion that I did not talk about much—not then, not now. I loved to dance. I joined a ballet class at the Alliance Française run by an English lady who was as strict as they come. Apart from a German boy, I was the only other male in class. Learning Western ballet was odd enough, but being a male student definitely brought forth some sniggers. And when I later decided to learn Bharatanatyam, the sniggers persisted.

I can recall vividly the first time I met my gurus, who would ultimately teach me so much more than

Bharatanatyam. It was their son U.K. Jayadev who facilitated this meeting. I have known Jayadev since my early days in theatre. In fact, he was one of the well-known actors of Bangalore Little Theatre. He invited me one day to Maha Maya to a very private gathering of artistes to see Sonal Mansingh perform the *ashtapadi*s from Geeta Govindam. I was transfixed. Here was an art form that integrated the essence of dance, drama and music as if they were never meant to be separate from one another. Sonal was effusive in praising her gurus whose presence at the concert added to the charm and magic of the evening.

Although well into their seventies by then, I felt the gurus were as radiant as the descriptions of Radha and Krishna made them out to be. Their youthful vigour and inner beauty were well preserved. Shri U.S. Krishna Rao had an enviably straight posture with a silver mane that made him look handsome and dignified. Smt. Chandrabhaga Devi, true to her name, was as resplendent as the moon. Photographs at one end of the room

23

showed them as young dancers. I have yet to see such beauty and grace!

Soon after my first encounter with them and the brilliant performance by their student Sonal Mansingh, I began to question my own limited understanding of the performing arts and how pale it was in comparison to what I had seen in that tiny performing space, so mystically named Maha Maya. In this 'Grand Illusion' I had had a glimpse of the truth in relation to art. Perhaps this was really my quest—to find some meaning in my limited range as a theatre practitioner with no real grounding. To top it all, I was handicapped since English was my medium. I had nothing except my passion.

I was determined now to learn from them. I felt a little awkward in asking them directly. After all, I was already in my twenties and they were the most sought-after gurus of Bharatanatyam with students from all over the world. So I enlisted the help of their son Jayadev. I called him one fine morning and came to the point. Would his parents consider teaching me Bharatanatyam? If

Jayadev was surprised or amused at my request, he certainly hid it well. He put me on hold but I could hear him talking to his parents. He explained to them that I was a theatre enthusiast. I could sense their hesitation and I heard Jayadev asking them to meet me at least. I was elated when they agreed to a meeting.

The six years I spent learning dance from them were my most formative years, both as a human being and as an artiste. My gurus could not make a dancer out of me, but they gave me the sense of discipline that set me apart from other theatre practitioners. They put me in touch with the richness of the classical tradition. I developed a greater spatial-temporal awareness. Basically, it opened my mind to all the tools needed for a dramatist; from the *bhava*s and *rasa*s to precision and rhythm on stage—I learnt all this from them. Even today, I go back to the basics of my dance training to further my understanding of theatre. This period also gave me something precious. I wrote my play *Dance Like a Man* out of my experience as an aspiring male dancer, largely inspired by my gurus, though the play is nowhere near a biography. The play went on to become the biggest success of my career to date.

People often ask me what the secret of my success is. Much of the secret still eludes me, but I can say that without a mentor it is impossible for anyone, no matter how talented, to find their way to success. Often creativity and talent require artistes to immerse themselves in their art—almost to the point of 'getting lost' to a certain degree. So without a mentor offering you direction, there is the danger of becoming too self-indulgent and hence counterproductive. I was lucky to have yet another mentor in my life—someone who, on first appearance, seemed quite the antithesis of everything I thought my dance gurus stood for (although later I was able to understand and appreciate their commonalities in dedication, professionalism and perseverance).

When I took my production of *Dance Like a Man* to Bombay, we had a very thin audience at the Sophia Auditorium. But among them was an important person—God. Alyque Padamsee was called God in advertising circles—and with good reason. He had made the careers of many luminaries in advertising and film. In the arts and entertainment industry, Sharon Prabhakar, Dalip Tahil, Shiamak Dawar and many others were all his protégés.

That night, God had come along with his wife, Sharon. Much to our delight, they came backstage after the performance and invited us all to dinner at their home, which was literally round the corner from the hall. Alyque asked me what I was working on next. I told him it was a play with a bizarre plot involving conjoined twins and their emotional separation over the years. He loved the concept and asked me to send him the first draft by post—this was, after all, the pre-Internet era of the late 1980s. Alyque put his secretary on the job and I wrote the play just to keep the secretary from calling me with reminders. I called the play *Twinkle Tara* and did a production of my own in

Bangalore for the Deccan Herald Theatre Festival. It was a huge success.

But more was in store. Alyque removed the 'Twinkle' and called it *Tara*. When Alyque chose to direct it, he had hoardings put up all over Bombay with my name just as big as his. God was promoting me! The press lapped it up and I actually got tired of giving interviews and posing for pictures. All this before the play had even opened. But after the high came a big low. In the theatre, many people, especially the English, consider *Macbeth* to be a jinxed play and call it 'the Scottish play' lest the mention of the play bring bad luck. Many laugh it off. But with *Tara* I can aver with proof that it was indeed jinxed—or at least Alyque's production was. The first calamity was that Alyque fell off the stage during the technical rehearsal and had to be rushed to the hospital. He had broken an arm. A car ran over producer Raell Padamsee's foot and she ended up with a good part of her leg in a cast. If both the producer and director with limbs in casts did not seem calamitous enough, something more tragic happened. Pratap Roy, a fine stage actor who was playing Dr Thakkar in the play, died of a heart attack soon after the third performance. It just was too scary. Maybe it was the severed 'Twinkle' from the title—who knows? But despite these mishaps, Alyque's production of *Tara* was a huge success and established me as a promising playwright, at least in the eye of the national media. Thank God, indeed.

By the time the 1990s rolled in, my theatre group, Playpen, was established and recognized in Bangalore. It was possible for me to move from one production to the next, confident that I would somehow manage to get a sponsor. I had begun work on my new play *Bravely Fought the Queen* and was putting the finishing touches to it when I got a call from Alyque. He asked me if I was aware of the motion in Parliament by the VHP (Vishwa Hindu Parishad) about building a temple in Ayodhya in place of the existing mosque. I was in my early thirties then, but as naive about politics as today's seventeen-year-old. This wasn't even headline news at that time and so had slipped my attention. Alyque was most concerned with the rise of religious fundamentalism and was certain of a pogrom brewing that would destroy the cultural harmony of the country yet again. I wasn't too sure of doing a play on the Hindu–Muslim divide. Sensing my hesitation he invited me to Mumbai and arranged an improvisation with Pearl Padamsee's students at the J.B. Petit school. The improvisation had two Muslim boys who, running away from a mob that is out to kill them, seek shelter in a Hindu household. The improvisation was riveting and I could see the dramatic possibilities.

It took me almost two years to write it. Again I was keen to do my own production in Bangalore first. But a week before the scheduled performance at the theatre festival, the Babri Masjid was destroyed. Although I had based my play on the Tazia riots in Ahmedabad in the 1980s, the play now took on a different shade. The festival organizers pulled the play out of the festival at the last minute.

It took another two years before it could be staged. An NGO in Bangalore offered to stage it. The tag line read 'A plea for tolerance'. But due to its initial ban, word had gotten around that the play was controversial. I was advised by friends not to do it, especially in the light of the Bombay riots. I remember, a whole section of the auditorium was filled with practising Muslims who were keen to see the play, and later I came to know that most of them had never been to a play before. The performance was met with silence. But the actors found themselves surrounded by new fans after the performance. Many of the Muslim members in the audience came backstage and congratulated the actors. They could not believe that the actor who had played Javed was not, in fact, a Muslim. Clearly, the actor was the hero. And I vicariously revelled in that heroism. When the actor politely introduced me to them, they showered me with gratitude for putting up the play. I even made a new friend who, till this day, continues to call me on and off just to inquire after my health and well-being.

I was deeply moved by the heartfelt response to my play. Perhaps it was this kind of unconditional acceptance that I craved for as a human being. Now I was ready to take on the world.

Critics, of course, pulled the play down, calling it weak and sanctimonious. One critic said that a middle-class Muslim boy cannot be so self-aware and articulate. In the same paragraph she said that the play is preaching to the converted! I could see how blind they were to their own prejudices. They were no longer important. I had found my validation amongst the ones who mattered— voiceless people like myself. This is what marked my departure as a playwright. I wanted my writing to explore areas that people wanted to be kept in darkness. In doing so, I was clearing the clouds that loomed over my life and my identity as a dramatist.

When Alyque subsequently produced it in Bombay, he had to put in his own money as no sponsors were willing to back it. Alyque was personally going through a bad patch. He was compelled to make a public apology for having spoken up against Bal Thackeray and the Shiv Sena. But Alyque continued to fight for peace and harmony in the country, and the city of his birth. His production was spectacular. He took the play to colleges and had feedback sessions. Some of these sessions went on longer than the play. Most young people could identify with the dilemma of the young characters. Older people met the play with some reserve. Many dismissed it as 'minority appeasement' (I wonder who had coined that dreadful term—a majority appeaser for sure!). Alyque believed in the play and that made all the difference to me. He taught me through his actions what my dance gurus had taught me through their dedication—that you must pursue what you believe in.

It was around this time that Lillete Dubey breezed into my father's office one fine day and told me about her theatre group in Delhi, where she lived. Apparently, the veteran playwright Mahesh Elkunchwar had suggested to Lillete that she look at my plays. Both my father and I were completely

33

struck by Lillete's exquisite presence in our humble little office. Later my father told me he was really happy with my involvement in theatre. He got to meet someone as beautiful as Lillete.

I forgot about our meeting soon after as I didn't hear from her. By this time, I was travelling abroad quite regularly on scholarships and exchange programmes. During one of these programmes—a particularly enjoyable teaching stint in the summer at Portland State University in Oregon, USA—I got a frantic call from my father that Lillete Dubey was trying very hard to reach me. I called her immediately and we ended up chatting for over an hour. She had begun rehearsals for *Dance Like a Man*! She wanted me to be present at the opening night in Delhi. I worked things out and managed to show up in Delhi on her invitation.

I thought back then that she would do four shows in Delhi and that would be the end of the story. And I strongly suspect that Lillete felt the same way about this odd play on Bharatanatyam dancers and their ruminations. The play surprised both of us and gained a life of its own, beyond our control. The rest indeed is history as her production continues to run even today—it soon crossed 500 shows, which is a rarity for English-language theatre in India.

Wherever I have travelled with the play, including cities in the West, I have always been asked whether the play is autobiographical, or whether my parents opposed my interest in theatre or learning Bharatanatyam. It struck me then how people can be so parochially literal when reading stories. They assume it is the author's own life story that they hear. As a result, they fail to see—let alone understand—his gaze. Or maybe it is to do with the assumption that 'eastern' writers 'tell their own story', whereas the sophisticated Western writers write from observation and insight. Both are stereotypes that many people, eastern or Western, buy very readily.

This was even more evident with my play *On a Muggy Night in Mumbai*. The play had its genesis in *Night Queen*, a short play that I had written for the *Telegraph Literary Supplement*, Calcutta, in the early 1990s. *Night Queen* deals with gay love, loss and betrayal. I developed it later, specifically for Lillete and her group. I knew I was stretching myself with this but I simply had to write it, especially after my experience with *Final Solutions* wherein I was able to reach out to and connect with the minorities I represented.

On a Muggy Night in Mumbai was received with dismissal mostly. On opening night, I could hear comments like 'It's a sick play'. An elderly couple were talking about how in the West 'this sort of thing is very common'. Most people chose to ignore it completely, as if they had never watched it. This was even more hurtful than a strong negative response. I first attributed all this to our society's conservative views on homosexuality. I remember Arnab Goswami called me for a chat show in which the subject of debate was 'Should we allow homosexuality to be depicted on our stage and in films?'. I am happy to note that the opinion poll that started with many a no swung in favour of a yes by the end of the show. But, surprisingly, the biggest dismissal vis-à-vis my play came from the budding lesbian and gay community. They hated it, and they hated me. Their accusation was that I showed gay men to be stereotypical. Even to this date, they refuse to acknowledge it as the first Indian play with gay love as its central theme. I must concede that my characters make too many political assertions, which may weaken the dramaturgy. But at that time, in the 1990s, any gay person who had the courage to be out had to be political, and I feel my characters were perfectly justified in standing up for their cause. I continue to stand by my play on those grounds.

Last year, I visited the Pride Library at the University of Western Ontario. They had a history of Indian gay drama and literature collated by members of a prominent LGBT community in Mumbai. Neither the play nor the movie version that I directed later had been listed. There is a line that I wrote for the movie version, where the central character asserts at the end of a tragic moment: 'They can't do us harm, any more than the harm we do to ourselves.' Again, I feel that this line resonates with most minority communities who often internalize hatred and turn it on themselves. Perhaps the weakness of the play lies in the fact that I failed to find the right metaphor to contain my characters' inner states and I made them too overt and direct. As such, the play may be limited by definition as a play of ideas and hence find its space as a problem play. It remains the least produced of all my plays, almost twenty years after I wrote it.

Years later, when I wrote *Seven Steps around the Fire*, a detective thriller set in the fascinating world of the hijra community, a group of hijras contacted me and expressed their gratitude for having represented them on stage 'so beautifully'. They were gracious enough to accept the failings shown in the play—failings of power play and interpersonal conflicts in their community, failings that they mirror from mainstream society. Once again I felt validated and accepted. I can't think of a more triumphant moment in my career apart from winning the Sahitya Akademi Award.

But *Dance Like a Man* continues, till today, to be my most successful work. It has even been made into a National Award–winning film by Pamela Rooks. To me dancing, singing or performing in general has always been a metaphor for living life to the fullest. Perhaps it is this metaphor that resonates most with audiences who love to see the play twenty-five years after I wrote it. This metaphor plays out in three of my works that I call my triptych.

The first of the trilogy is, of course, *Dance Like a Man*. Dancing, in the play, represents the ideal world, almost impossible to attain in one lifetime. Yet it is a world that the protagonists strive for at all costs. The second of the triptych is actually a film. *Morning Raga* is about music that unites different worlds—the past and the present, the young and the old, the traditional and the modern. Music heals. Music crosses bridges and borders.

Life is complete with the singing of a song that needs to be sung. The third one is *Where Did I Leave My Purdah?* It explores the life and travails of Nazia, a stage actress who has lived a life in the theatre for sixty years. The play is a tribute to the great actresses of company theatres, who were courageous enough to pursue their passion for the stage at a time when stage actresses were looked down upon. For this I have as my inspiration the legendary Zohra Sehgal. Again, the play is not a biography, but somewhere the spirit of the doyenne lives in Nazia.

Dance, music and now the world of the theatre—the triptych unites them all. Time and memory are important elements that provide a plot to my plays, so there is some irony in the fact that a huge time gap separates the writing of these three works—two plays and movie. There are at least twenty-five years between the first work and the last.

Now when I look at the triptych as a whole, I feel that a part of me has come to rest. In some strange way, I have imbibed the idiosyncrasies of my characters and in singing my song, or dancing my dance, or playing my role, I have a sense of accomplishment. Not artistic accomplishment, which is a constant endeavour, but one of the spirit. I am now hungry to move on and find another person in me, a new playwright maybe.

Perhaps the reason why I chose dance, music and drama as my metaphors is because I wanted to live vicariously through my characters since I am not an accomplished dancer, singer or actor. But there is another very strong link between these three plays, one that has been vital to their success. The link is none other than Lillete Dubey. *Dance Like a Man* did not choose her but she chose *Dance Like a Man*. I then chose her to play an important supporting character in *Morning Raga*. And, finally, *Where Did I Leave My Purdah?* chose Lillete. It would have been impossible to write the play had it not been for the fact that I knew she would play the part. Nazia was born to be possessed by Lillete.

Mahesh Dattani

The relationship between a playwright and an actor is a complex one. Both rely on one another for their artistic fulfilment. Again, each lives vicariously through the other's creation. Each one is the artist for the other, just as each is also the other's muse. For that I am eternally grateful for the presence of Lillete Dubey in my life.

Having put my dancing demons to rest, I move on. I moved to Mumbai in 2005 soon after my mother's death. The city of Mumbai embraced me—particularly Ashvin Gidwani, one of the biggest producers of theatre in Mumbai. For him I wrote my response to the city that I have grown to love and hate with equal passion. *The Big Fat City* is a play that may have all the elements of a knockabout farce but is in fact a black comedy on the sad, lonely but stimulating lives that we lead in this city of dreams. Even as I write this essay, the play is running before audiences that are used to seeing full-on comedies. They haven't decided yet what to make of *The Big Fat City*. But over the years I have discovered that time is the only decider

42

of a work's endurable merit. I simply surrender to my time and place, and hope to change as a person and as a dramatist.

I have learnt to embrace change as the only way to survive in the world. Today the world is filled with new ideas and new art forms emerging from the use of technology. Theatre too is moving out of the proscenium and speaking more intimately with its audience. I may be dated in some ways (I still believe in the classic design of a play), but my gaze has moved away from my own little world, and I now look for new meanings and definitions in the kind of theatre we have in the cities today. Often I am disappointed when I see tired adaptations of older plays, or the absurd fixation young English-speaking actors have with the Theatre of the Absurd. But ever so occasionally I watch a new piece by a young group not afraid to express themselves, and know that we are on the verge of exciting breakthroughs in our arts. That is when we will truly find our identity as the new face of an ancient civilization.

And no matter what, nobody can take away the dances you have already had. That is a quote from *Where Did I Leave My Purdah?*, but actually Gabriel García Márquez had said that. I use this quote at the moment, very early in the play, when my protagonist Nazia Sahiba decides to go back to the theatre after a gap of thirty years, still craving for more dances at the ripe 'young' age of eighty-two! I think it is fair to say that my own reflections on my time in the theatre find an echo in Nazia's bold proclamation: 'I want more dances. Dances that nobody can take from me. Oh! This van is too small! It can't take my dancing. Your cinema is too small for me. My life is big. I am BIG and GENEROUS. Only the theatre deserves me!'

Mumbai   Mahesh Dattani
5 August 2013

Where Did I Leave
My Purdah?

A Stage Play

A Note on the Play

Mahesh and I share a *junoon*, an all-consuming passion called theatre. It maddens us, delights us, frustrates us, exhilarates us, nourishes us, and agonizes us, in equal measure. But it also imbues our lives with a special meaning and lights it up, literally and metaphorically!

So it was a natural corollary that we would one day want to tell a tale set in this nebulously unreal (yet in so many ways much more real) world, and put it on stage. To try and share our peculiar and

Facing page: Soni Razdan as Ruby and Lillete Dubey as Nazia in the play. (*Courtesy Natasha Hemrajani*)

mystical fascination with it. And thus was born
the kernel of the idea for *Where Did I Leave My
Purdah?*, a story set against the backdrop of the
theatre, tracing some of the theatrical forms that
constitute our history, and recounting a tale that
mirrored the stories of a multitude of women
artistes who were consumed with a love for their
craft, almost at the cost of everything else. These
were dynamic women who were driven by a
deep compulsion to fulfil their artistic needs, in
spite of the fact that their work would live only
ephemerally in memory.

And so was spun the story of the irrepressible,
irreverent, iconoclastic and utterly human Nazia,
who is inspired by a legion of Amazonian legends
that have blazed across the stage, living, loving and
even sacrificing all for their art. Mahesh, with his
talent, took the play two steps further—instead
of merely setting it against a theatrical backdrop,
he gave the story more power and depth by
heightening the tension and placing the core of the

story during the Partition, with all its upheavals and far-reaching consequences.

On a personal note, I found the play a delight to direct and perform.

As a director on account of the structure: The present, the past and the play within the play (where we rediscover a classic, Kalidasa's *Shakuntala*) flow seamlessly into each other, but with their own individual rhythms and beats. Each segment mirrors and echoes the other, the whole coming together like one piece of music, underlining the trajectories of the protagonists on many levels, including off the stage and on.

As an actor, because of Nazia's role—that of a feisty, passionate, self-absorbed diva: Now which actress worth her salt wouldn't want to play that! Especially when the playwright says he wrote it just for her. And the fact that my daughter Neha played young Nazia—to my old—was a uniquely poignant and strangely moving experience.

The play reaffirmed my belief that we constantly

underestimate audiences, believing that they are wary of new material and forms and are looking mostly for work that makes little demand on their grey cells. Audiences have responded to the play in an amazing way, understanding with ease the different time zones and realities the play operates within, and have enjoyed thoroughly the challenge of connecting the dots and unravelling the various threads of its non-linear structure. When you have chosen a path where you constantly want to explore and stage new material, this is a wonderfully heartening reaction.

If they are ready to dive in and test those untested waters with you and go back challenged and excited, this junoon must be getting something right!

Lillete Dubey
Founder, The Primetime Theatre Co.

Where Did I Leave My Purdah? opened on 27 October 2012 at TATA Theatre, National Centre for the Performing Arts, Mumbai, with the following cast.

NAZIA SAHIBA	Lillete Dubey
RUBY / ZARINE	Soni Razdan
SUHEL / KING DUSHYANT / FIRST ASSISTANT DIRECTOR	Siddharth Makkar
YOUNG NAZIA / SHAKUNTALA / NIKHAT	Neha Dubey
YOUNG ACTRESS / GAUTAMI / SHAKUNTALA'S SAKHI	Priyanka Karunakarann

Mahesh Dattani

Producer and Director	Lillete Dubey
Lights	Bhola Sharma
Sets	Lillete Dubey and Bhola Sharma
Original Music	Gandhaar Sangoram
Photographs Courtesy	Natasha Hemrajani
Costumes	Trishna Popat
Graphics	Mamta Somaiya

The playing time of the first production was eighty-five minutes without an intermission.

Scene I

The vanity van of Nazia.

The door opens slowly to reveal a handsome young man in his late twenties. He comes in with some reserve. His name is Vinay. It is a bit dark and the curtains are drawn.

VINAY. Ma'am? . . . Ma'am, sorry to disturb you but . . . Are you asleep? . . . Ma'am? . . . Your shot is ready.

He draws open the curtains. He looks around and notices Nazia lying on the floor. He panics.

VINAY. Oh fuck! Oh no! (*Calling out*) Security!

Vinay goes to the body on the floor. Nazia is

53

a wrinkled, frail woman in her eighties. She is dressed in a white sari and wears a wig, a grey one with a grandma bun. She looks like the quintessential widowed dadi maa of television and Bollywood movies.

Nazia comes around and lets out a series of gasps. Vinay quickly gets her some water. She gestures she doesn't want any. She motions that she wants to get up. Vinay tries to help her up. She clings to him. Vinay's cell phone rings. He can't answer it.

Nazia's breathing is more forced now. Nazia goes limp in his arms. The cell phone continues to ring. Vinay rests her on his knee and gives her mouth-to-mouth resuscitation.

NAZIA. And that is how Sleeping Beauty woke up.

VINAY. Oh no! Oh, ma'am! How could you?

NAZIA. Answer it. Answer it.

VINAY (*on phone*). Hello. Yes! I am coming! She is ready. (*To Nazia*) Ma'am, please hurry, the shot is ready.

Nazia has gone to a video camera.

NAZIA. I win the bet! I win the bet! You know, I told Waheeda that I will have you in my arms kissing me as if it were a matter of life and death. She owes me a lunch at Wasabi.

Vinay's cell phone rings again. He cuts the call.

VINAY. Ma'am, please! Ranbir, Deepika and Rishi sir are all on the set. Sanjay sir is screaming!

NAZIA (*checking out the video*). Let him. Let them all scream! Ah, Waheeda was so sure she would win. Wait till she sees this video. Nanda too! She thought you would rather die than . . . But I knew you would do it. Those girls are in for a surprise . . .

VINAY. That was not fair. You took advantage.

NAZIA. It's okay. I know you are gay.

VINAY. I am not gay! Who told you that?

NAZIA. Nobody told me. I know.

VINAY. But I am not!

NAZIA. Oh no! You poor boy. You don't know you are gay!

Mahesh Dattani

Vinay's phone rings again.

VINAY. Yes, yes! She is coming! What can I do? I can't carry her, can I? . . . Okay. Okay.

Vinay hangs up and looks at Nazia with serious intent.

VINAY. Ma'am. If you don't come for your shot now, my orders are to carry you there.

NAZIA. You wouldn't dare! Go tell that boy Sanjay I want him to come here and escort me.

VINAY. He won't come. He is taking Rishi sir's close-ups now—

NAZIA. Hah! Rishi sir's close-ups! Tell him Rishi's grandfather used to come to my green room and escort me—now see. See what you made me do. You made me live in the past. Okay. Okay. I know that Sanjay adores me. But Chintu needs his close-ups I guess. (*Adjusting her wig*) Let's go. By the way that spotboy is no good. He couldn't remember a thing I said. I sent him away. What are my lines?

VINAY (*opening the door*). Just one line. '*Yeh sab kya ho raha hai, beta?*'

NAZIA (*aghast*). Noooo! Not possible! I thought that line went with Leela Chitnis. I told him! I told Sanjay he needs to be different. (*Picking up her Galaxy*) See, I sent him an email. This scene is just before the climax! Read it! Read it!

Vinay squats on the floor in frustration.

VINAY. Why me? Why me?

NAZIA. I will read it out. You should have your eyes checked. Maybe you need glasses.

Nazia picks up a huge magnifying glass to see her screen with and scrolls down on her phone.

NAZIA. Here is the mail I sent him. 'Dear Sanjay, about the family scene—I feel it needs more punch. Since I am the matriarch I feel I need to deliver that punch. I need to gather everything so that the audience can recall the plot. Times have changed and you need to recap . . .' (*To Vinay*) Nowadays they have the attention span of a sparrow so you need to make it snappy.

Vinay's cell phone rings.

57

VINAY. Ma'am . . . S-Sanjay sir.

NAZIA. Ah Sanjay! Talk of the devil. (*Taking the phone from him*) Sanjay darling, you didn't read my email . . . Yes, I am ready beta and waiting for hours, I was waiting for your Assistant Director to call me, but he was busy bonking the watchman. Let me read out my mail to you and explain the scene to you . . . this scene leads to the climax so you need to gather the plot. Audiences have the attention span of a . . . (*Sanjay has interrupted her. She listens very carefully.*) Oh, so you did read the mail . . . okay. You want me to say '*Yeh kya ho raha hai beta*' . . . and nothing more . . .

Nazia hands the phone back to Vinay.

VINAY (*hurt*). You told him that I was—bonking the watchman.

NAZIA. This is it. There's always a time in your life when the truth strikes you. (*A moment of realization for her*) Why didn't I see it? What am I doing here? I don't belong here! (*Taking off her wig*) No more grandma roles for me. I am going back to the theatre! Dancing! That's it. I am leaving.

VINAY (*with folded hands*). Please! Leave. I will tell them you hit me with your broomstick.

NAZIA (*ripping off her sari and wearing her kaftan*). I don't need this shit. That's what I told them when they wanted to give me chemotherapy. I don't need this shit. And I survived! Yes, I don't need this—

(*Begins to dance using her sari as a veil*)

No matter what, nobody can take away the dances you've already had. You know who said that? . . . Márquez! He and I danced once in Rome. I want more dances. Dances that nobody can take away from me. Oh! This van is too small! It can't take my dancing. Your cinema is too small for me. My life is big. I am BIG and GENEROUS! Only the theatre deserves me!

CROSS-FADE.

Scene II

The vanity van opens out to become a ramp for a stage. The stage is mostly bare except for a few chairs. But at one side is a whole stack of trunks, the kind used by theatre companies to store properties.

Nazia is still dancing, now to a captive audience, a young aspiring actress.

NAZIA. All that space to fill with your body and your voice. Letting those feelings flow to fill the hall right to the last row of the balcony. And to have a good time doing it! That is the magic of theatre!

Nazia finishes her little dance with a flourish.

The actress applauds.

ACTRESS. Ma'am, may I have a picture with you?

NAZIA. Later, later. You are here for auditions first. You must keep reminding me that you are here to try out for my new production. If you give me half a chance I will show off.

The actress laughs politely.

NAZIA. Now don't look like a scared rabbit. I am just trying to give you an idea of what I am looking for. You see, I am looking at a revival of *Abhigyan Shakuntalam*. It was the grandest production in our repertoire. But we have done all that Kathak stuff. It's nice, I am not saying it's bad. But it's done. Been there, done that. We are doing it for today. What do young people want to see? Something snappy. I downloaded some stuff from the iTunes store. And look what I found.

Nazia finds the music on her iPod with the help of the huge magnifying glass. She plays some trance music with sitars and tabla.

NAZIA. There. Can you dance to that?

The actress moves to the music and then begins to dance. Nazia joins in as well, completely involved in getting the best out of the actress.

Unknown to them, Ruby, a woman in her sixties, is watching them. Ruby is wearing a loose, flowing kaftan.

Nazia notices her and pulls the iPod out of its dock.

NAZIA (*going to her*). Ruby!!! Oh, my darling Ruby.

RUBY (*embracing*). Hello, aunty. How are you feeling?

NAZIA. Don't call me 'aunty' in front of these kids.

RUBY. But you are my aunt.

NAZIA. Nazia! (*Saying the name grandly*) Nazia Sahiba! Call me Nazia, or 'ma'am' if you wish.

RUBY. I think you would prefer 'ma'am'. So I will call you Nazia.

NAZIA (*taken by surprise*). You never called me Nazia. It was always 'aunty'.

RUBY. But you just said you didn't—

NAZIA. Of course I want you to call me Nazia. I hate being your aunt.

RUBY (*with some bitterness*). That I know!

Silence.

NAZIA. Anyway, let me finish with this kid. (*To the actress*) Okay. Let me tell you something about my theatre company. You have heard of the Modern Indian Theatre, right?

ACTRESS. Yes of course!

NAZIA. Who started the Modern Indian Theatre?

ACTRESS. You did. You did, ma'am.

RUBY. Hah!

NAZIA. I along with a few others.

RUBY. Others? Others?

NAZIA (*deliberately avoiding looking at Ruby*). Nineteen forty-six. It is sixty-five years old.

ACTRESS. Yes, we learnt about that at NSD.

NAZIA. All over. It was great stuff. But now it's your turn to do great stuff. We will do a modern version of *Abhigyan Shakuntalam*. Here is a poster design I thought of.

Nazia holds up a poster mock-up with the title SHAKU! in metallic blue.

This does take them by surprise. Nazia deliberately waves it in Ruby's direction and then places it on an easel.

Ruby laughs.

RUBY. Others!

ACTRESS. But, ma'am, what is the old version about?

NAZIA. Brilliant! I like the younger lot. Couldn't care less for the past. Well, you don't really want to know. You won't come with any baggage then. *Abhigyan Shakuntalam*, the Recognition of Shakuntala. In a nutshell, it's about this beautiful young woman who grows up in an ashram in the forest.

ACTRESS (*dreamy*). Shakuntala! I love the name.

NAZIA. Yes. And she—

Ruby's phone rings. Nazia throws her an annoyed glance.

NAZIA (*saccharine sweet*). Bye, Ruby dear. Thanks for dropping by.

RUBY. I am not going yet. We need to talk.

Ruby takes her call, speaking softly, but her presence still irks Nazia.

NAZIA. Then there is this gorgeous hunk of a king. King Dushyant. He happens to be hunting and spots Shakuntala with her friends. Hormones run amok. They secretly marry and then he has to leave. But he gives her his ring, assuring her he will send a royal entourage to escort her to the palace. Goodbye. But then a sage puts a curse on Shakuntala that whoever she is thinking of will forget her.

ACTRESS. Oh my God! She was thinking of the king! But why did he put a curse on her?

NAZIA. You know how sages are! All they can do is curse. We must have a movie director in our version . . . He felt offended because she didn't get him a glass of water . . . But then when his anger subsides, he adds that the curse can be revoked by presenting something the person has given her.

65

So Shakuntala is consoled that when she shows Dushyant the ring, he will recognize her.

> *Ruby laughs. Nazia glares at her. It is*
> *unclear whether Ruby was laughing at what*
> *the caller said or she is listening to the story.*

NAZIA *(gesturing as if putting a curse on Ruby).* I curse you. You don't exist . . . Well, that was worth trying . . . Anyway, a pregnant Shakuntala is taken to the palace and of course Dushyant fails to recognize her because of the curse. So Shakuntala wants to show him his ring. But, alas, the ring is not on her finger. It slipped off and fell in the river when she was praying.

ACTRESS. Oh no!

NAZIA. So she is humiliated at the court of the king. She cannot go back to her father's hermitage either. After she leaves, a fisherman finds the ring in the belly of a fish and hands it over to the king. It all comes back. The memory of Shakuntala. But she is gone!

RUBY *(butting in, having finished her call).* She was pregnant when she left the king. Do you know my mother played that part in 1946? (*To Nazia*) Tell her that.

ACTRESS. This is so powerful! Ma'am, I want to play Shakuntala.

NAZIA. We will see.

ACTRESS. You know when a role is meant for you! I can see this one is for me.

RUBY. Everyone wants to play Shakuntala. Only one woman is lucky enough—to play it for forty years. Making sure no one else will.

NAZIA (*ignoring Ruby, to the actress*). Okay. Here's the good news. I like you. But I don't know whether you can play Shakuntala.

ACTRESS. I will do anything for that part!

RUBY. Even kill someone?

Nazia stares at Ruby.

ACTRESS. Yes! It's a part to die for! Even to kill for!

NAZIA (*to the actress*). Let me see. Tomorrow come with your thoughts on what it feels like when you recognize someone. Truly recognize a person. What does it mean to you today? That's

67

what *Shaku* is about.

The actress nods with enthusiasm.

NAZIA. Okay. Now scram.

The actress touches Nazia's feet.

Ruby laughs again.

The actress leaves.

RUBY. You know, you could have had the decency to at least mention her name.

NAZIA. As if mentioning her name will make you happy. You are unhappy because you choose to be.

RUBY. I am not talking about my unhappiness. I am talking about decency.

NAZIA. I am too old to be decent now. (*Doing a hip roll, humming* Shaku-la ka baby *just to annoy Ruby*) Now, are you going to help me with the costumes or not?

RUBY. You started the company together. How can you just fail to mention that the company was founded by both you and your sister?

NAZIA (*wandering around*). You know, you have

really let this place go to seed. I allowed you to have your embroidery workshop here but you hardly ever come here. I can tell. Cobwebs! I hate cobwebs . . . What are these?

Nazia tries to open one of the trunks.

RUBY. Will you please, in future, show the courtesy of mentioning my mother? I know this is going to bring you a lot of publicity. 'Nazia to revive the Modern Indian Theatre.'

NAZIA. 'Post-Modern Indian Theatre'—that's its new name. Now what's in these?

RUBY. They are my new exhibits. I sent you an invitation.

NAZIA. But why? Nobody is interested in these moth-eaten costumes. They will laugh at them. I would laugh at them now. They were awful. So kitschy. No, don't open them. I don't want to see them.

RUBY. This is history! (*Throwing open some trunks*) *Yehudi ki Beti . . . Bahadur Ladki . . . Jasma Odan . . .* and . . . and . . . (*Removing her kaftan.*

69

Mahesh Dattani

*Underneath she has on a costume of a forest
dweller as seen in* Shakuntala, *knotted bodice,
midi-sari and flower bracelets*) Shakuntala.

Nazia stops in her tracks.

NAZIA. Where did you get that from?

RUBY. Not from your warehouse for sure! And
you know that!

NAZIA. I know that! That is why I am asking
you, where did you get that from? Oh, it doesn't
matter, probably from Shamshad, that seamstress's
daughter. She seemed like she would keep these—

RUBY. I got them from Suhel Uncle.

Pause.

NAZIA. Suhel? That old fool is still alive?

RUBY. Why not? You are. Old fool! That's really
rich coming from you who—

NAZIA. I know I am old. But I am not a fool. He
was a fool even when he was young. (*Picking up
her cell phone and giving a voice command*) Call
Dipti. (*While holding her phone, speaking casually*)
Where is this Suhel guy?

70

Ruby laughs.

RUBY. Go on. Pretend it doesn't matter. I know it does. He is in an old-age home in Delhi. Can't walk, needs help . . .

NAZIA. (*on the phone*) Dipti? Darling, will you send one of your office boys to my Jogeshwari warehouse? There is a lot of junk over here that I want cleared . . . Old clothes and stuff. He can burn them. Not give them away, but burn them, do you hear? . . . Good. What a wonderful secretary you are! By the way, don't let Sanjay or his AD know where I am . . . Love you. Bye.

RUBY (*disturbed*). You can't do that.

NAZIA. This is my warehouse and these are my trunks. I should have done this years ago. See, this is what comes of giving you my space. And get out of that ridiculous costume or I will burn you along with it.

RUBY. This is mine. I know this belongs to me! My mother wore this, didn't she? . . . Suhel Uncle gave me a few other things. (*Rummaging in the trunk and producing a photograph*) See this. Does this jog your memory? Though I suspect it doesn't need much jogging. Here she is. That is Shakuntala and this is her costume. My mother.

NAZIA (*looking at it with her magnifying glass*). Lahore, 1948. That is Zarine. Yes. You are wearing her costume. But this is not Shakuntala's costume. I was always Shakuntala.

The lights fade as music, natya sangeet of the 1940s, plays.

The vanity van is now a green room of the 1940s. We see the young Nazia and Suhel (played by the same actor who plays Vinay). They are dressed as Shakuntala and Dushyant.

Suhel creeps up from behind and embraces the young Nazia warmly. Nazia leans back and pulls Suhel's face closer to her and they kiss.

A backdrop of a forest scene rolls down, hiding the props of the previous scene.

Scene III

We are in Lahore, 1948, soon after Independence and just when the horrors of Partition are being felt. We start mid-performance of the dance drama Shakuntala *in Hindustani.*

The play begins with a dance scene where Anasuya is played by Nazia's sister, Zarine (played by the same actor who plays Ruby). Anasuya is dancing with Priyambada. They carry pots.

At an opportune moment in the music, the beautiful, young Nazia moves from the green room and appears centre stage. There

73

is a mild applause on her 'entry'. They dance to the music and singing that describes Shakuntala's beauty and their innocent frolics in the forest.

Unknown to the ladies, King Dushyant is observing Shakuntala from behind the tree.

Towards the end of the song, a bee appears to trouble Shakuntala. Her dancing turns wild as she avoids the bee.

Shakuntala is troubled by a bee.

SHAKUNTALA. Upset by the drizzle of water falling on its body, this bee is hovering around my face instead of the jasmine.

DUSHYANT. Oh, black bee! You are truly fortunate, for you are being watched by her restless glance. You are touching this trembling young woman again and again, humming close to her ears as if trying to tell her a secret.

SHAKUNTALA. Oh! This wicked bee does not give up! (*Going to another spot*) Oh! Has it come here too? What should I do now? Friends! Save me!

74

Anasuya and Priyambada giggle.

ANASUYA. Who are we to save you? And why don't you call for King Dushyant? It is the king's duty to protect this sacred grove.

SHAKUNTALA (*still troubled by the bee*). Oh, what do I do now? Who will save me?

Dushyant suddenly appears in front of Shakuntala and splits the bee in two with his sword.

DUSHYANT (*going to Shakuntala*). The black bee will not trouble you any more.

They look into each other's eyes. Shakuntala looks shyly away, trying to conceal her excitement.

The two look at each other. An awkward silence.

A gun is fired. Screams among the audience. Pandemonium breaks out. The actors are scared as well. Shouts of 'Maar dalo un haraamion ko!' 'In sab ki talaashi lo!' 'Stage pe kaun hain?' 'Chalo! Sab Musalmaan

ja sakte hain!' 'Kafiron ko pakdo!' *etc. A
commotion.*

Suhel brings the women together.

SUHEL. They are coming here. Quick! Into the
green room!

They move to the green room.

More shouts backstage. 'Koi Hindu hain
yahan? Nikalo bahar sab ko!'

Gunshots and more screams.

NAZIA (*to Suhel*) They are coming for you! Quick!
(*To the girls*) Wear your burqas! Hurry! And give
him a cap.

*The girls quickly wear their burqas and
Suhel wears a Muslim prayer cap.*

*While they wear burqas, the woman who
played Priyambada mutters.*

WOMAN. We should never allow Hindus in our
troupe.

NAZIA. Shut up! Not a word!

WOMAN. This can never come to any good. Hindus

must leave! Go to India. This is no place for you.

SUHEL. I won't let any harm come to you on my account.

More gunshots and screams.

NAZIA. I will handle this. (*Shouting to a mob*) There are no Hindus here. Only us artistes.

MAN OFFSTAGE. We know the kind of plays you put up, prancing around naked on stage. And then you move around with that Hindu. Whores like you will find no place even in Hell!

Suhel is angered, he runs backstage to tackle the man. A scuffle.

NAZIA. Suhel! . . . Leave him alone! Leave him alone, please!

SUHEL (*offstage*). Nazia, leave! Go home!

Suhel screams in pain as he is being beaten up.

Nazia gets a gun from her vanity bag and goes backstage.

ZARINE (*terrified*). *La hawla wala quwwata!*

A gunshot.

Silence.

Nazia re-enters with the gun.

Zarine begins to cry.

ZARINE. Ya allah! What have you done? You killed a man!

NAZIA. Quiet, Zarine.

Suhel enters.

WOMAN. They saw your face! You did not cover it! Those men who ran away, they will find you, Nazia.

SUHEL. The three of you go home.

NAZIA. And you?

SUHEL (*taking the gun from Nazia*). I will take the blame.

WOMAN. There is a train going to Delhi tonight. Take that train! You won't be safe here.

SUHEL. She is right, Nazia. Once I reach Delhi, I will ask you to join me.

ZARINE. That will never happen. Abu won't let you!

NAZIA. I am going with you, Suhel. Now.

SUHEL. No. It's too dangerous.

NAZIA. I don't care. I would rather die with you than live without you.

They embrace.

SUHEL. Quickly. Get out of your costumes. They will come looking for him. My uncle will get us on the train. Hurry up. I will pack a few things and try to get a tonga. Come to the back street as soon as you hear my whistle.

Suhel exits.

WOMAN. Nazia, you can't leave! What will become of the group here?

NAZIA. It is up to you, Shamim. Come to India if you want or stay here and forget about drama.

WOMAN. How can you just leave the land of your birth?

NAZIA. So you made your choice! You want to stay here, so you clearly value that above the theatre company. For me the company is the most important thing!

WOMAN. I don't know! I don't think you are doing

the right thing. Have some fear of Allah! . . . And what's the point in going with you? I know you won't let me play Shakuntala!

Woman exits.

Zarine and Nazia are alone.

ZARINE. Abu won't let you!

NAZIA. We are not going home. Get into your clothes. You are coming with us.

ZARINE. No! I—I can't. I want to go home to Ammi and Abu.

NAZIA. Zarine. They are waiting to do your nikah with that attar-wallah's son. Do you want that?

ZARINE. No, but . . .

NAZIA. Come with us, Zarine. We will go to India! We can set up our own company theatre there. You do want to do that, don't you?

ZARINE. Yes, but . . .

NAZIA. Look. Once we are there and we set up our company, you can play Shakuntala. OK?

ZARINE. Can we go home first and at least speak to Abu?

NAZIA. Don't be so foolish! Always dithering. For once in your life make a decision that will do some good. Obedient girls like you always end up in unhappy marriages . . . Well, you make up your mind now. (*Taking off her burqa*) I am going, and there are no two ways about that. Either you come with us or you stay here all by yourself.

Nazia makes to leave. Zarine is rooted, not knowing what to do. Nazia stops.

NAZIA (*quietly*). Zarine. I didn't think twice about killing that man to save my Suhel. Anyway, I will write to you.

As Nazia is about to leave . . .

ZARINE. Nazia! I will go with you!

NAZIA. Then hurry up! Find a trunk and take all that you have! Quickly!

Nazia leaves.

Zarine looks around.

The sound of a steam-engine train slowly leaving a station.

ZARINE. Goodbye Lahore. My city. Please forgive

Mahesh Dattani

me, Ammi, Abba. Forgive me! I will take care of
Nazia. The Koran is a witness to that.

The train picks up momentum.

FADE TO NEXT SCENE.

Scene IV

We are in the present now, back in the warehouse. The older Nazia is alone and on her cell phone.

NAZIA (*on the phone*). Hi Dilip! How are you, my dear? All well with the new marriage? . . . Good. I am glad it's working out—finally. If it doesn't I can set you up with this really handsome assistant director . . . Listen, did you go through my proposal? You know, the *Times* is planning to make this a cover story. My revival of the Modern Indian Theatre. *Shaku* is going to be all over town—along with the P.K. Wineries logo. Why don't you give away a free bottle of your lovely Shiraz to everyone there on premiere night? . . . Oh. You did? What did your MD say? . . . He doesn't want a modern version? . . . You mean—you won't sponsor it? No, I don't want to do the original. He can take it or leave it . . . Okay! And tell him his Shiraz tastes like a mix of vinegar and cow piss anyway! . . .

Nazia hangs up, muttering to herself.

She doesn't notice that Vinay has come in and is waiting patiently for her to notice him.

NAZIA (*on phone*). Dipti. Dipti darling, these are desperate times. You don't happen to have a sponsor as a client, do you? . . . I thought as much. Well, tell that movie producer I will do that grandmother role for a crore . . . I know, I know, nobody pays a crore for a grandmother. It was worth trying. Maybe I should get Deepika to play Shakuntala. That will bring in all the sponsors. Darling, get me Deepika's number. Oh, shoot. I was supposed to be shooting with her and—

Vinay's phone rings. Nazia notices him.

VINAY (*mumbling into the phone*). I have reached. Will call you back.

NAZIA. You! Dipti darling, I will call back but do think of something.

VINAY. Ma'am, I am not leaving unless I take you back to the shoot. I have orders to bring you to Vaishno Devi right away. It's the climax scene!

NAZIA. What do I have to do? Ring bells?

VINAY. Yes. You are praying for your grandson's recovery. Sanjay sir is calling you right now and you better take his call. You might as well deal with this issue now. I am not leaving unless you go with me!

NAZIA. Then don't leave.

VINAY. I am warning you, I won't. Please, ma'am. They will fire me if I don't bring you.

NAZIA. And it's been your dream to be an assistant director. Or you are madly in love with Sanjay.

VINAY. I am not gay.

NAZIA. You don't know it. I do.

VINAY. Look, I have a girlfriend and she will tell

you that you are wrong. I mean, whatever gave you that idea. Do I look gay?

NAZIA. So your dream is to assist Sanjay. Is that what you are saying?

VINAY. Nobody dreams to be an assistant for anything. I am an actor. FTII, 2006.

NAZIA. And you are hoping Sanjay will take you in his next film. You think, one day, Hrithik is late for a shoot and is fired, and Sanjay turns to you and says 'Assistant, you play the part'. That's your fantasy, isn't it? Hah! Fat chance! Not possible in films, but in the theatre! In the theatre you can dream for anything to happen! Stick around . . . What's your name?

VINAY. Vinay.

NAZIA. Dash! You will make the perfect Dash.

VINAY. Dash?

NAZIA. Dushyant of old. I thought of Dush but Dash is more—dash.

VINAY (*a little wary*). What do I have to do to get the part?

NAZIA. Just be—yourself. You are perfect. For the part.

VINAY. And then—you will go to Vaishno Devi?

NAZIA. To ring bells and pray for my grandson—I know, I know. I will deal with that too.

VINAY. You have to deal with it right now! Why don't you finish one thing before starting another?

Nazia's phone which she has left on a table starts to ring. The ringtone of the phone is an electronic, disembodied voice saying 'Unknown calling, unknown calling'.

VINAY. That's Sanjay sir!

NAZIA (*waving at the phone, continues*). You see, Dash doesn't quite know Shaku—

VINAY. I suggest you answer it first, then you can tell me about Dash.

NAZIA. Don't you want to know more about your role?

VINAY. Ma'am—

NAZIA. What kind of actor are you?

VINAY. Please answer the—

NAZIA. To me the role is everything! Worth dying for!

VINAY. Please, ma'am!

NAZIA. Worth living for!

VINAY. It is important that you answer your phone and speak to Sanjay sir.

NAZIA. He can wait! I can't! I want to get on with *Shaku*!

Vinay goes to the phone and answers it.

VINAY. Hello, sir, she is here, I will— (*Realizing it is not Sanjay*) I am so sorry. Yes, she is. Just a moment. (*Holding the phone out to her*) It's for you. No, it's not Sanjay sir.

NAZIA. Who is it?

VINAY (*on the phone*). May I know who is speaking? . . . (*To Nazia*) It's a gentleman called Suhel.

Beat.

NAZIA. I don't know any Suhel.

After a while Vinay speaks to the caller.

VINAY. She says . . . You heard, okay. Look, she is busy now and— (*After listening for a while he speaks to Nazia*) He says he is Suhel—your husband.

NAZIA (*shouting for the benefit of the caller*). I don't know any husband! He heard that so why don't you just hang up?

VINAY (*going to Nazia, taking charge*). Whatever it is, finish it. Then we go to Vaishno Devi and after the shooting is done we come back and do your play, okay?

Pause.

The sound of a train rumbling through a tunnel.

NAZIA. You think it is so simple? . . . Things don't get finished. They just hide in a dark corner like a ghoul and grab at you when you are not looking. And sometimes you have to beat the shit out of the ghoul to make it crawl back into its dark corner.

The sound of a train coming to a screeching halt, metal dragging on metal.

NAZIA (*grabbing the phone, putting on a stern voice that trembles occasionally revealing her turmoil*) Hello, have you hung up? . . . Why didn't you? . . .

> *While Nazia listens she is aware that Vinay is most curious about her conversation. She turns to Vinay.*

NAZIA. Vinay darling, why don't you get my handbag from my car. The driver is standing right outside. But get it yourself.

> *Vinay understands and leaves. Nazia braces herself for a talk with Suhel.*

NAZIA. Did you say Ruby gave you my number? . . . you didn't say. But she did. What do you want from me? Some money? . . . I am not trying to be insulting, just practical. You are sick and in hospital and could do with some cash, right? . . . Oh, good for you that you have sons who will pay for all that. Where are they? New Jersey or somewhere, and they send you a couple of hundred dollars every month and call you and say 'I love you, Dad' . . . Where? Birmingham? Same thing. I don't really care . . . Look, stop babbling. You are babbling . . . You are not making any sense . . . Why do you call after fifty bloody years? To tell me you have sons in Birmingham? . . . But why? . . . Well, I don't want to see you. Sorry about that . . . Oh, so you can still read. Yes, I am reviving the company. Is that why you want to come? So you can take credit for everything you didn't do? . . . Well, you left me to handle the company on my own. I—look, let's not even go there . . . (*Warning him*) Don't bring her into this . . . You will what? . . . If you say anything to the press I will . . . Just leave her out of this . . . Are you blackmailing me? . . . Good, because I don't want to see you . . . You can say what you want to the press . . . No! Don't come here. Please! . . . I don't want to see you because I will feel sad to see you in a wheelchair! I will feel sorry to see you holding a bag filled with your own piss! I cannot even bear to hear your shaky voice now. You are just a phantom.

In the vanity van area, we see the young Suhel and Nazia dressing up to play Dushyant and Shakuntala.

NAZIA. We are not who we were. And I think it is a good thing. Of course I wish I were as beautiful as I was. And I wish you were too. We were both beautiful but—what's the point now? It's over. No point. Cobwebs.

The old Nazia exits.

FADE TO NEXT SCENE.

Scene V

The early 1950s. The young Nazia and Suhel are putting on their costumes and accessories in the make-up room for the post-intermission act. At the same time the set for ACT III of Shakuntala *is put up.*

SUHEL. Where is my armlet?

Nazia points to a box even as she puts on her make-up.

SUHEL. And can you please try and show a little more feeling in this scene? I am declaiming my love for you and you just stiffen up.

Mahesh Dattani

NAZIA. I don't stiffen. Shakuntala has never been touched by a man before that.

SUHEL. Well, look into my eyes at least.

NAZIA. She wouldn't. She is too coy.

SUHEL. Yes, she is coy, not . . .

Suhel checks himself.

NAZIA. Not what?

SUHEL. Repulsed. Why do I feel that you find me repulsive?

NAZIA. You noticed it now?

SUHEL. What is that supposed to mean? Are you saying—?

NAZIA. Never mind.

SUHEL. What is it?

NAZIA. Let's just get on with the rest of the play, please! We can talk later.

SUHEL. When? After the play you will be surrounded by the group. You will rehearse with them till morning. Then when I am too tired to talk, you will quietly slip into bed and go to sleep. When will

94

we get a chance to speak about what is bothering you? Nazia, you need to come out with it.

Silence.

SUHEL. Look, a lot has happened to us but we need to—

NAZIA. To me! A lot has happened to me! Nothing happened to you!

SUHEL. I know. I know that, but don't you think it has affected me as well? I try not to show it because I don't want to upset you.

NAZIA. It shows!

Pause.

NAZIA. Why is it that when you play Dushyant— especially this scene—I feel that—you are accusing me?

Pause.

SUHEL. Maybe because I am a good actor . . . Or maybe not. Maybe I should stop playing Dushyant then.

NAZIA. Yes, maybe you should. Jagan is more than willing to take over.

SUHEL. Oh, so you've been rehearsing with him, have you?

NAZIA. You can play the role as long as you like.

SUHEL. But you'd rather I didn't.

NAZIA. Yes. You can do that for me, can't you? After all, I left my home and family for you . . .

Pause. Suhel comes over to her side.

Nazia stiffens.

SUHEL. That's not entirely true, is it?

NAZIA. I don't care if you believe it or not.

SUHEL. You do care. If I don't believe it, you won't have anything to hold against me.

NAZIA (*throwing a lipstick in his direction*). Wear your caste mark. It's come off in all your sweat.

SUHEL. You left Lahore because you knew you will have a better chance of starting your company here. I know. Shamim told me you said so.

NAZIA. Why are you all so cruel to me? I am trying my best to make ends meet for all of you. Applying for grants, going through the accounts, training actors . . .

SUHEL. Is it the company you care about? Or the roles you play? Jasma Odan, Shakuntala. You choose the scripts with care making sure you have the meat, while you feed the rest of us the bones!

NAZIA. That's why I don't want to talk to you. You just doubt everything that I do!

SUHEL. You never gave your own sister a chance to play Shakuntala. She was talented and far more suited to play this role.

The first bell goes off.

NAZIA. Get ready. The interval is almost over. This is your last performance. I can never perform this with you as Dushyant after what you just said!

SUHEL. But that is the truth. Don't you think Zarine would have made a good Shakuntala?

NAZIA. She would make a great Shakuntala. But she isn't here. So what's the point? And I don't want you talking about her!

SUHEL. There is a point. If she were here, would you have offered her that role? It is easy for you to say 'Oh, my poor sister. She would make a

97

great Shakuntala. Too bad she is dead.' And you promised her you would let her play it.

Nazia can no longer control herself. She begins to cry.

SUHEL. Oh good. So you *can* cry. That is what I want. Put more feeling into your role. And some into our relationship.

NAZIA. I will if you stop being so cruel.

Second bell goes off.

SUHEL. I just want you to come out of yourself and look around. We are all victims of our time. I sympathize with what happened but—

NAZIA. I know how you, Rati, Chandra and the others look at me. I don't need your pity. It is so easy to put someone down by pitying them and you don't miss any chance of doing that to me!

SUHEL. I don't pity you, I want to help—

NAZIA. Oh, so I am helpless! And I need you to help me? So you can take control over my life. Oh, there are too many women in dance and theatre who have succumbed to those tactics. Too many who allowed men to ruin their lives. But I am not one of them. I certainly don't need your help in bringing about my destruction!

SUHEL. Yes, you do need help! For God's sake, move on!

NAZIA. Move on? I am trying—trying to do that, but you keep reminding me of what happened . . . I just have to look at you and it all comes back! I can't play Shakuntala because of you. The first time I see you as Dushyant, I look away because it reminds me that I once made the mistake of falling in love with you. When you kill the bee it reminds me that I killed for you. When you take me in your arms as Dushyant I—I want to throw up!

SUHEL. But why? What have I done or said that makes you feel this way?

NAZIA. It's what you didn't do.

SUHEL. I am trying to cope with this as well.

NAZIA. No. You cannot believe that you went through the same hell. That is not true!

SUHEL. You are right. It is not the same . . .

NAZIA. And in the court—when you spurn me, the look in your eyes! You mean every word you say! I know where that comes from. It all comes back! I cringe at your touch. When you reject me in the court, I wish I could wipe out every memory of you, Zarine and . . . and . . . everything else!

The final bell rings, a long one this time. Nazia hurries to the door. She hesitates.

NAZIA. I don't know how I am going to survive this scene. How I wish I could just put my arms around you to wring your neck instead of pretending to love you! I can't love you any more.

SUHEL (*unbelieving*). You still blame me for what happened?

NAZIA. You did nothing to stop it! Nothing!

Suhel begins to understand for the first time what she is going through.

SUHEL (*softening*). If that's the way you feel I will hand over the role to Jagan from tomorrow's show onwards. I—I am leaving you, Nazia. I am leaving you—alone. You don't need me. You want to forget the past? I am your past. I was hoping we would have a future together which could somehow heal both of us . . . I hope the company will give you the solace you seek. I converted to Islam to marry you. I can now leave you under the same law. So . . . talaq, talaq, talaq.

Suhel exits the green room and goes on stage, taking his position on the throne.

Nazia, almost in tears, puts on her ghagra which has a false belly attached to it. She now looks six-months pregnant.

As she gets out of her green room for the scene—

An apparition of Zarine dressed as Shakuntala, holding an infant, appears in front of her.

The sound of a train whistling by.

Zarine smiles. She rocks the baby in her arms to the rhythm of the moving train.

Nazia takes in a sharp breath.

ZARINE. You promised me I can play Shakuntala. What a lovely baby Shakuntala has! A real prince.

No—princess. Of royal blood! Blood! Blood! . . .
(*Gesturing, to go on stage*) But it's okay. You can
play the part since I am not here. Play the part.
Play it well!

Nazia is frozen.

SUHEL. Come on! Take your position.

ZARINE. Call me Shakuntala for once.

SUHEL. They are waiting to open the purdah!

NAZIA. Shakuntala . . .

ZARINE. Oh, thank you, sister! Now play the part.
Forgive Dushyant. He is, after all, a man. They
forget . . . Take care of the baby. Rabiba. What a
lovely name! She is all yours! Only yours!

> *The apparition of Zarine disappears. The
> sound effect of the train fades away.*
>
> *The lights come on stage.*
>
> *A pregnant Shakuntala stands before
> Dushyant in court. Shakuntala wears a veil
> that covers her face as she is in a courtroom.*
>
> *An elderly lady, Gautami, has brought
> Shakuntala to the court.*

GAUTAMI. Arya! I bring a message from the hermitage. Since you have married this noble woman under the Gandharva tradition, without consulting elders, you must now make public your marriage and accept Shakuntala, who is carrying your child in her womb, as your wife.

DUSHYANT. What are you talking about? I don't understand these words of marriage.

Pause.

GAUTAMI. O King Dushyant, choose your words carefully. People pass disrespectful comments about the woman who, howsoever chaste, is not accepted by her husband when she is pregnant with child.

DUSHYANT. Try as I might, I do not recall such an exchange between this woman and I.

Shakuntala raises her veil and turns to the king.

SHAKUNTALA. Look at me and say you have not married me under the Gandharva tradition.

DUSHYANT. Respected lady of the hermitage! I

A theatrical effect used in the 1950s with quicklime underlined with music. A quick burst of fire and a smokescreen. Shakuntala vanishes.

As the smoke clears we see the old Nazia clearing cobwebs, coughing.

FADE TO NEXT SCENE.

Scene VI

NAZIA. God! Look at all this dust. Does anybody clean this place? Hello! Is anyone around? Where is that one-legged, half-witted cleaning boy I hired? What's his name? (*Pulling at a cobweb*) Look at these cobwebs! No matter how often I clean them all, they keep coming back. Next we will have Spiderman swinging around! Why on earth are all these files still here? What's this? (*Picking up a large portrait of Shakuntala covered in newspaper. She unwraps it*) Oh my God! This is still around. (*Yelling out*) Hello, you halfwit! Throw this in the bonfire as well!

Ruby enters.

NAZIA. Rabiba dear. I am terribly, terribly sorry, but Dipti's man came, took all those wretched costumes and burnt them. You must have seen that right outside. So much smoke. Didn't expect those old bits of satin and zari to burn so much . . . I am so so sorry . . . I just couldn't bear the thought of those glittery things hanging on dummies. Neat little labels describing the play and the probable year, and too bad you won't be winning some little award for it or a grant from the IFA or some such thing. No coffee-table book for me to release next year with lots of pictures. Too bad they are gone now . . . (*Doing a mock wiping of her hands*) Over. Finito. Khatam.

Ruby does not respond.

NAZIA. What? Aren't you going to scream at me and call me a heartless bitch?

Ruby laughs.

NAZIA. Don't laugh.

RUBY. You really think I would let you burn away my mother's memory? I knew you were planning to destroy those costumes. So I called Dipti and explained to her the importance of those costumes. She understood and said she will send her guy over and get him to burn some old newspapers just to humour you, and hand over the costumes to me for the exhibition! So I have them, safely in my car. My driver is guarding them, with instructions to look our for a certain cute old lady who might trick him into parting with them.

NAZIA. I will burn your car down! They are mine. You have no right.

RUBY. They are of national importance. You have no right to destroy them.

NAZIA (*yelling*). Who the hell are you to tell me that? Don't forget who I am. And this is my warehouse. I got you that post as costume historian using my influence! Your London School of Fashion diploma wouldn't get you anywhere! I gave all those recommendations, and now you tell me I have no right? Go, get those damn costumes out of your car right now and put them in the bonfire!

RUBY. I have a sponsor for you. Do you want to do your play? You will have to do as I say then.

NAZIA. You are such a manipulative little bitch.

RUBY (*losing it*). Oh, nowhere near you, Nazia Sahiba. You are the mother of all bitches! You manipulated everyone who was unfortunate enough to be part of your life. Why do you think none of the old guard is here today taking pride in the revival of their company?

NAZIA. They are not here because they are all dead. Bhola is around. He is doing my sets.

RUBY. If his father were around he would have warned him against working with you. They all left you. I know. Suhel Uncle was the first to leave you, because he knew you better than anyone else!

NAZIA. Why are you so concerned with the past? If you had a present like I do, you won't be thinking of all these things. Things didn't work out with you and your husband either. That doesn't mean you are a manipulative bitch. You are one, I know, but not because your husband dumped you. Does your son hold you responsible for what happened?

RUBY. I have a daughter, not a son.

NAZIA. Whatever. That's not the point.

RUBY (*picking up her bag*). I know you want me out of your life, but I am not going anywhere until you acknowledge my mother's work publicly! Once you do that I will let you go.

    Leaving.

NAZIA. Okay. If it will make you happy, I will attend your silly exhibition and I will acknowledge Zarine's help.

RUBY. Not simply acknowledge her help, but give her credit as a co-founder of the company. I am going to appeal to the Sangeet Natak for a posthumous award for her. But first it has to come from you.

NAZIA. I will do it. If you have a sponsor for me.

RUBY. Tell me something. (*Going to her*) Is Suhel Uncle my father?

NAZIA. Everyone thinks so.

RUBY. But you would know. That explains why you don't want to talk about my mother or your husband. Maybe you were angry at them for having an affair. Is it true?

NAZIA. I don't know.

RUBY. Do you or do you not want to do the play?

NAZIA. Show me that you have found me a sponsor.

RUBY. I should have realized what would interest you. (*Pulling an envelope out of her bag*) Just to assure you I mean what I say, I got the winery to put it down in writing. I just said it will have a slightly modern interpretation and left it at that.

Nazia is ecstatic.

NAZIA. Oh, just wait and see. It's going to be a kick-ass production! I just need to find a Shakuntala.

RUBY. You had hundreds coming in for the auditions.

NAZIA (*reading the letter*). I have found a great actor for Dushyant. Dash. But Shaku . . . If only I were younger by sixty. (*Excited*) You see, this is the interpretation I always wanted for Shakuntala! Not this whiny little creature whose entire future depends on whether her husband can remember having slept with her or not.

RUBY (*lost in thought*). So you haven't found your Shakuntala yet. How interesting.

NAZIA. I will, I will. When is the first cheque coming? I need to pay Bhola an advance and I need to get the music rights to some of that— (*Noticing a card along with the letter*) What's this?

RUBY. That's for you. That's the invitation for the inauguration of the festival—

NAZIA (*checking with her glass*). Have you put my name in bold?

RUBY. As requested by you.

NAZIA. What's this? . . . Are you mad?

RUBY. What are you talking about?

NAZIA. This! You must really hate me . . .

RUBY. Your name is up there, in bold!

NAZIA. You've invited him as well!

RUBY. Of course! He was part of the company whether you admit it or not.

NAZIA. He dumped me and the company!

RUBY. He did not! He did not dump you! He told me.

NAZIA. He must have gone senile by now. What would he remember?

RUBY. A lot more than you.

NAZIA. You want me to sit with him on the same dais? After fifty years? And you think it is okay?

RUBY. About time, don't you think?

NAZIA. What do you get out of tormenting me? What do you want?

RUBY. The truth about my parents! I want to hear it from both of you.

NAZIA. He is not your father. Your mother is dead. And I don't know who the hell your father was. What more do you want to know?

RUBY. That's the story you want me to believe.

NAZIA. It's the only story there is!

RUBY. Like Dushyant, maybe you have forgotten something. Maybe a little memento would remind you.

NAZIA. You are getting old and senile before me. A memento! Like what? A ring maybe?

RUBY. Something like that. I will get the truth out of you if it is the last thing anyone gets out of you!

Nazia is about to respond, but the young actress enters.

ACTRESS. Sorry, ma'am. Sorry, traffic problems.

NAZIA. Same here. Everyone wants to go zipping through my memory lane as if it were a highway to nirvana! (*To Ruby*) It's a dead end! (*To the actress*) Okay. So did you do your homework?

ACTRESS. I love the way the script is developing.

NAZIA. Good. I am glad we are on the same page. Now let's see how the scene goes. Okay, so this guy in black is jamming when Shakuntala walks in. His guitar goes crazy when he sees you. (*Going to her iPod*) Then you—improvise the rest. Okay?

ACTRESS. Yes, ma'am.

NAZIA. Okay. Shaku, go out. When I yell 'enter', you come in.

The actress exits.

Ruby has been observing all this.

RUBY (*leaving*). Excuse me. I think—I know what needs to be done . . .

Ruby leaves.

NAZIA (*muttering after her*). Well, good for you. Okay. Let's switch off some lights for some mood. It's a dark den of iniquity. A regular Mumbai rave party.

The lights are dimmed.

She plays her iPod. Guitar strumming. As the music builds up—

NAZIA (*yelling*). Enter!

The woman does not enter. Nazia pauses the music.

NAZIA. What's the matter?

ACTRESS (*offstage*). So sorry, ma'am. Sorry.

NAZIA. Okay. Let's start again.

The music plays as before.

NAZIA. Enter!

Again the woman fails to enter. Nazia pulls

the iPod out of the dock.

NAZIA (*yelling*). Do you want my hearing aid? Who are you talking to over there? I know you have the attention span of a sparrow, but—concentrate!

ACTRESS (*offstage, a little nervous*). I—I am so sorry, but . . .

NAZIA. This time if you don't enter when I tell you to, you are fired! Now pay attention to my cue.

Plays the music again.

Just as Nazia is about to say 'enter', a figure approaches from the shadows.

Nazia picks up her magnifying glass.

The start of the steam engine, leaving the station slowly.

The figure approaches as the music and the sound of the train build up. We see it is Nikhat, a young woman in her twenties. She is Ruby's daughter. (Note: To be played by the same actor playing the young Nazia/ Shakuntala.)

Nazia looks at her and is startled.

NIKHAT. Hello, ma'am. My mother thinks I might help jog your memory a bit.

A shrill blast of the train whistle. The sound effect of the train is cut—

Dramatic music from Shakuntala *takes over. Spotlight on Dushyant holding the ring. In the spotlight is the sketch Nazia laid out earlier. The older Nazia is also fixed in a spotlight.*

DUSHYANT. It comes back to me now! How could I have forgotten the time I spent with Shakuntala? After seeing this ring, all those memories tumble through my mind like a waterfall without any banks. They pound at my mind, like the look in her eyes when I rejected her, inflicting wounds on my soul! Dearest Shakuntala, I am burning with repentance for having deserted you. Soothe my wounds by forgiving me and return to me, with my child! (*Holding the painting*) I have drawn your beautiful face so that I feel you are here beside me. Yet your beauty has not completely descended on this sketch. Let me complete this picture so that I may live.

Dushyant exits with the picture.

Back to the present, Nazia is visibly shaken.

Actress enters a little nervous.

ACTRESS. I am sorry, ma'am. Ruby Aunty asked me not to enter so—

NAZIA. Never mind. Rehearsal's over, you may go.

ACTRESS. I am sorry. Please, ma'am, one more chance! I know I can play Shakuntala. Maybe it's the modern version I can't understand. But the original one—it makes sense. A woman does want her child to have a father. She does forgive the man for his shortcomings. Please let me play her!

NAZIA (*staring at her*). Tomorrow. Now just go. Takhliya. Scam. Shoo.

The actress leaves, fighting her tears, thinking she has failed the audition.

NAZIA. You did that on purpose.

NIKHAT. It was Mom's idea. While I was waiting, she told me to walk in with the music. I didn't mean to startle you.

NAZIA. But she means to kill me . . . She knew I

119

will get a shock seeing you. You look just like . . .

NIKHAT. Like Zarine Nani, I know.

NAZIA. No! I was going to say . . . like . . . Where have you been all these years?

NIKHAT. I am glad you ask. Was in the States, living with my dad. Studying theatre at Yale. I am on your fan page, if you care to check. I am just one of about 60,000, I know. I know you don't want to see me, but I need to—When I read about your plans—I wanted to audition for Shakuntala.

NAZIA. You want to spy on me, that's what you want to do. Your mother has set you up for this.

NIKHAT. It was my idea to audition. It was Mamma's idea that I visit Suhel Uncle first.

NAZIA. Why is everyone suddenly after that senile old man?

NIKHAT. Because, just maybe, he might be my grandfather.

NAZIA. Rubbish! Ask him, he will tell you!

NIKHAT. I did. And he said—yes.

NAZIA. Not true!

NIKHAT. He told me a lot of other things, which you will deny of course.

NAZIA (*on guard*). Really? What did he tell you?

Pause.

NIKHAT. He gave me some stuff. Let me bring it here.

Ruby comes in. She looks as if she has been crying.

NIKHAT. Mom! What's wrong? . . . Who were you talking to on the phone now?

Ruby just stares at her.

RUBY. I—never mind . . . Nazia, this is Nikhat, your grand-niece.

NAZIA. Your daughter, yes, I know.

RUBY. Don't you think she will make a great Shakuntala?

NAZIA. Spot on.

RUBY. You agree?

NIKHAT. It's like my grandmother has returned—to claim her role.

121

Nikhat goes out to bring her bag.

RUBY. Yes! Oh my God, yes! Oh, what a story it will make! And what greater way of giving my mother her due credit! (*To Nazia*) Except, you have to comply to make it happen. The press will want to hear it from you.

Nikhat enters.

NAZIA (*in a daze, still looking at Nikhat*). Yes. Except . . .

NIKHAT (*removing a poster from her bag*). But first, there is something that I have to say which you are not going to like, ma'am.

Nikhat pins up the poster on the easel that has the poster of Shaku. It is an original lithograph of the 1950 production of Shakuntala with a huge picture of the young Nazia. The credits have been blanked out.

Nikhat stands next to it. The resemblance is clear.

NAZIA. He had this poster?

NIKHAT. Yes. He said he saved it from your

destructive hands. That you were hell-bent on destroying everything.

NAZIA. What else did he say?

NIKHAT. He told me. He told me that—it was Zarine who played Shakuntala, not you!

Silence. Nazia is lost in thought.

RUBY. You mean, she is lying? That is *my* mother? In the poster?

NIKHAT. He said—It was Zarine who took over Shakuntala once we came to India.

RUBY. But it makes sense! Look at you! You are the spitting image of your grandmother. It has to be her. (*To Nazia*) And how clever to blank out the names on the poster. So that is why you don't want to face me. You don't have the courage! Who is to know what really happened sixty years ago? Everyone is dead. And when they were alive they were too scared of you. So they let you take all the credit after my mother died. On and on you go about playing Shakuntala. You still want to hang on to that stolen glory by reviving the play with your twisted interpretation. I won't let you now. I will reveal how devious and crooked you are. You will be stripped of all your awards. Your name will be mud.

NAZIA. Zarine died much before those revivals.

RUBY. . . . Everyone said my mother died after giving birth to me. Everyone said that because that's what you told them. I wonder now! You are capable of anything! I could kill you right now for destroying me. How I hate the sight of you. Even as a little girl, being handed over from an actress backstage to a seamstress to the washerwoman. They fed me all right. But I was only a pair of hands that could sew or mend or bring in cushions and flowers or hand over a bouquet to the chief guest. Even then I hated you. I could see you in your green room putting on make-up. I would wait for someone to open the door so I could catch sight of you. You only looked at yourself. Never at the world around you. I didn't exist. Everyone sympathized with me. Poor girl, her own aunt does not want to look at her. Send her to her uncle. No, no, he is married again. His wife will not want her

. . . I hate the theatre, I hate my father for deserting me like this, but I hate you more than anyone else. You were so close to me and yet you may as well have been thousands of miles away.

NIKHAT (*going to Ruby*). Mom, I know it's hard to let go.

RUBY. I wish . . . (*To Nazia*) Life would have been so different if you had died instead of my mother!

NAZIA. Yes. Yes!

NIKHAT (*firm with her mother*). Mom! I know, I know it hurts, but there is no point in taking it out on her.

NAZIA. Let her! Let her take it all out on me! I can take it! Come on! Spit it out.

> *Ruby is about to say something. Nikhat interrupts.*

NIKHAT. Mom! No. Don't.

RUBY. You don't know, Nikhat! You can never know what it feels like to be abandoned as a child.

NIKHAT. I do. I do! I was just as angry at you, Mother!

RUBY. I didn't abandon you! You haven't been through the hell I have. I made sure you didn't.

NIKHAT. I held the same anger against you. You didn't notice my anger because—you were too angry yourself, at your mother for dying and leaving you.

Silence.

NIKHAT. You gave what you got. Oh, you were always around at home, trying to compensate and making sure I didn't go through the same feeling of abandonment. But even when you were holding my hand waiting for the school bus to pick me up, you were thousands of miles away. Other mothers talked to their daughters. Asked about their homework, their teachers, their friends, but you never did. There was that whole week when you would give me my lunch box without packing my lunch in it, and at lunch break, I would open an empty lunch box. You went through the motions all right of being a caring mom. But you weren't. You couldn't. I was angry too. You didn't know this but Dad took me to a therapist in New York.

She helped me see that you were not to blame. Dad too helped me see that. He understands that your anger came out of your own unhappiness. It's okay, Mom, to let go. I am trying very, very hard!

RUBY. Nikhat, I—I didn't know. I am sorry but I just didn't know! I deserve the same punishment then as she does.

NAZIA (*looking at the poster*). The names—on the poster of the shows in Delhi—were removed because of the riots. We were afraid to reveal our Muslim names.

NIKHAT. Tell me that's not my grandmother in the picture! Look at me and look at the picture. What does it say?

NAZIA. I think that deep inside you know the truth. Your mother knows the truth. But we don't want to acknowledge it. We all weave these tangled webs around the truth so we can strangle it and make it disappear. We are all deceiving one another.

RUBY. You killed your sister.

NAZIA. Yes, I killed her. But that's not what I mean

127

. . . And, yes, Suhel is right. It was Zarine who played Shakuntala.

NIKHAT. How could she?

NAZIA. It was me on stage, but every moment on stage I could only think—this is Zarine's role. I promised her this role . . . I just couldn't forget her. When I played the part, she always took over.

The sound of a steam engine starting. A blast of steam.

NAZIA. I killed her, but no one sees it that way. I know I did. She died on the train.

The rhythmic motion of a train leaving a station and picking up speed.

Spotlight on Nazia. Nikhat and Ruby move about as young Nazia and Zarine. Suhel joins in.

NAZIA. The entire train was filled with Hindus migrating to India . . . The train to Delhi from Karachi. The infamous Flying Mail 9 Down. Yes, we were on it. We boarded the train at Lahore. Zarine, Suhel and I.

*We see Zarine, Suhel and Nazia with two
trunks huddled together. The green room is
now a railway compartment.*

NAZIA. The family beside us shared their food with
us. Zarine told them we were Muslims and Suhel
was Hindu, but they didn't seem to mind. The
train stopped just before we reached the border.
We didn't think much of it, until—

*Suhel, Nikhat and Ruby stand up motionless,
deadpan.*

NAZIA. Until we heard. Screams and—

Gunshots. A long piercing scream.

NAZIA. The rioters wanted to kill everyone on the
train. A train full of Hindus. Except for us. The
woman next to us told us to wear our burqas. That
would save us . . .

*Suhel wears a cap. Zarine and the young
Nazia open their respective trunks. The
young Nazia rummages inside her trunk.
Zarine takes out hers.*

NIKHAT (*as young Nazia*). Quickly! Wear your
burqa. Where did I leave mine?

The young Nazia looks elsewhere. Zarine puts her burqa in Nazia's trunk.

ZARINE. It's right here, Nazia! In your trunk! Wear it quickly.

More gunshots and screams.

The young Nazia wears the burqa quickly. Zarine helps her.

NIKHAT (*as young Nazia*). Why haven't you worn yours? (*Shaking Zarine with urgency*) Hurry, Zarine!

Zarine just stares at her, smiling.

Nazia slaps her.

NIKHAT (*as young Nazia*). Move! Wear it, you stupid girl! For once in your life think fast! Your life depends on it. They are coming! Where is it? (*Suddenly, looking at the burqa she is wearing*) Oh no! Zarine . . .

NAZIA. She gave me her burqa! She was always the one who was uncertain. She was always afraid of making a wrong decision! But now—she did not think twice! There was no doubt in her mind. Why did she do it? I didn't deserve it! What had I done for her that she should give her life to save mine?

Gunshots and shouts.

Ruby/Zarine slowly walks away from Nikhat and Suhel.

Constant gunshots and screams even as the older Nazia speaks.

NAZIA. Later, when Ammi wrote to me, I came to know. She—she had promised our parents she would look after me . . . She swore by the Koran that she would take care of me.

ZARINE (*waving goodbye*). Goodbye, my sister! Do well! Make a name for yourself. Let your dreams be fulfilled! Inshallah, I will see you one day in Paradise!

A gunshot.

NIKHAT (*as Nazia, screaming*). Zarine! No!

Suhel takes away a hysterical young Nazia.

Zarine comes back into the present space to become Ruby once again.

NAZIA. The butchers were on her and all the others.

Suhel dragged me away. We walked all the way to the border. We crossed the border after bribing someone. But . . . you see . . . I was still wearing that piece of black cloth. But we were in another country, with a different set of demons. They came at us. They came at me. They pushed me down behind the bushes. Five or six or seven, eight of them. I don't know. They tore at my clothes and at my flesh. All I could think of was why isn't Suhel saving me? These are his people! I stopped looking at those eyes, so much anger and hatred! Hell-bent on humiliating me. I stared back with hatred too, but they hurt me even more till—I stopped looking into their eyes.

A woman walks by with a bloodied face, limping. It is not clear if she is Hindu or Muslim. She lets out a dirgelike wail, which stays through the scene.

The young Nazia walks in wearing a tattered burqa. In a daze. She looks around.

NAZIA. The train arrived from across the border. Filled with bodies. On the train was written in blood: 'A present from Pakistan. For all the wrong you have done.' Blood from maimed bodies spilling out of the train. Suhel went first, to the bogey we were in. He couldn't—he couldn't tell who was Zarine. Even her clothes were bloodied. He called me . . . I saw her hand. On her finger . . . the ring with the inscription from the Koran. I recognized the ring. I recognized Zarine. Only just then. She was killed by her own people. I . . .

Nazia does a gesture to suggest she may as well have killed her with her own hands.

The woman with a bloody face walks by again. She looks at the young Nazia.

The young Nazia looks around.

NAZIA. I looked around for a shroud. I had to find a shroud for her before the mass burial. She would have liked a kafan.

The young Nazia looks around and is about to ask the woman, but she is too caught up in her own grief. The woman begins to sing a lullaby holding an imaginary baby.

*The young Nazia removes her burqa and
gently lays it down.*

NAZIA. A shroud for my sister. I buried her in that.
Never worn a veil after that.

The young Nazia exits. The lullaby continues.

*Ruby is moved by this. The old Nazia goes
to her. They are together in one spotlight.*

NAZIA. I knew you weren't Suhel's child. Although
we married, I couldn't hide the fact from him.
He said he would bring up the child as his own,
but—maybe it was me—every time he came close
to me I could see that look in his eyes, I could sense
it in his touch. Somewhere, we had forgotten each
other . . . We only remembered the pain.

*The woman leaves, her lullaby turning to
sobs.*

NAZIA. You were born . . . I didn't want to hold
you. I couldn't look at you, without all that coming
back! You were my flesh, wounded, humiliated. I
didn't cry when you came out. I was relieved—that
the tapeworms infesting my belly, left by those pigs
who ate at my flesh, were out of my body. When

Suhel gave you to me, I could not hold you. I told him to take you away from me! He thought that if I held you everything would be all right. He persisted and I resisted. He did not understand that if I held you—that I could just take my veil, wrap it around your neck and snap that tiny neck—get rid of you and my pain. Not because I hated you, but because I hated myself . . . Even today when I look at you . . . it comes back. I tried really hard to forget. I tried. And I will keep trying. Help me. Just leave me alone!

RUBY. I . . . I didn't know . . . I am sorry!

NAZIA. No! Don't do that! Don't pity me. Hate me. I will never acknowledge you as my child. I never want to! When we revived the company I told everyone you were Zarine's child. That she died during childbirth. You must learn to hate me for the rest of your life. I don't want your pity.

RUBY. I . . . I knew you were my mother . . . I hated you all the more! This morning . . . I spoke to him at the hospital. Suhel Uncle told me something that you don't remember yourself . . .

The young Nazia comes into the green room dressed as Shakuntala. She tiptoes to where the baby is.

RUBY. He told me that between acts and when no one was looking . . .

The young Nazia picks up the baby and suckles her.

RUBY. That you would suckle me . . . and Suhel Uncle would delay the next act to give you time to make sure I was well and asleep.

The young Nazia hums a lullaby softly, rocking the baby in her arms.

NAZIA. He—told you that?

RUBY. Yes.

NAZIA. Did he actually delay the next act? Because . . . to give me more time with you?

RUBY. Yes.

The young Nazia sings. The older Nazia is touched by the memory.

NAZIA. Do you think he will—forgive me?

RUBY. He already has. A long time ago.

NAZIA. Maybe I should—call him. Now. Or wait till I meet him?

RUBY. Mother, he died this morning.

Nazia backs away, unable to deal with this.

NAZIA. Why? I was doing fine until you brought it all up again! Why can't you all just leave me in peace? I have a production to plan, don't you know? Where are those actors? Vinay!! Get ready. We are going to start rehearsals in ten minutes . . . We are going to do the scene when they first meet—no, no, let's not do that. We will do the scene where he leaves her . . . no! No! . . . Let's do the scene where he insults her saying he is not the father of her . . . Or the scene where he recognizes her but . . . Let's not do *Shakuntala*, let's think of something else . . . (*Noticing the poster of the old* Shakuntala) Who put this damn thing here? I am doing *Shaku* not *Shakuntala*. Get this out of here! Burn this!

Nazia topples the easel on which it is kept. She backs into an old trunk and trips. She lets out a sharp cry of pain.

137

Ruby rushes to her mother, lying down in agony.

NAZIA. Aaaaaaah! It hurts!

Ruby kneels down and holds her mother to her chest.

NAZIA. It hurts! Zarine! Zarine!

Nazia clings on to Ruby, crying like a child.

RUBY. It's okay. It's okay, Mother. It's okay. It's okay.

The young Nazia rocks the baby in her arms.
Ruby rocks her mother in her arms.

NIKHAT (*as Nazia*). Go to sleep. Sleep, my child.

FADE TO NEXT SCENE.

Scene VII

Immediately, a spotlight picks up Vinay amidst a round of applause.

VINAY. Thank you, all. Working with Nazia ma'am has been a life-changing experience. I have learnt this from ma'am that theatre is about recognizing who you are . . . For some lucky actors, you find a role that kind of defines you in the eyes of the audience . . . You will see me in Nazia Sahiba's next production of *Romeo and Julian*. And I play the part that defines my life in my own eyes. Julian. Proud to be Julian . . . But, without further ado, let me call upon stage the person who made this production happen, without whom none of us would be here today. Ladies and gentlemen, our producer, Ruby Thakur!

Ruby enters amidst applause.

Vinay exits.

RUBY. Thank you. Doing *Shaku* has been an enormous task. Not only the hardships of putting a play together in a world that believes the art of the theatre is dying, but also for personal reasons . . . Too personal to talk about here. But, truly, I can say that there is no one as remarkable, bold, courageous and, above all, honest a person as my . . .

Ruby finds it difficult to go on. She contains her feelings with a slight laugh.

RUBY. —I don't want to keep you from the shining star behind the Modern Theatre.

NAZIA (*yelling from offstage*). Post-Modern Theatre! Get that right!

RUBY. It gives me great pleasure to call on stage, the one and only Nazia Sahiba!

Vinay brings in Nazia in a wheelchair. A sheet covers her from the waist down. A huge applause for her.

NAZIA (*beaming at the applause*). That's right. Give me more. All right. All right. You think you can pack me off with a shawl, a citation and a standing ovation? Not a hope! (*Pause*) This play is dedicated to Suhel. The finest artiste I ever met. And the most loving husband a woman could possibly have. (*Looking skyward*) Suhel, you and I have a lot to talk about. But don't hold your breath. I don't plan to join you yet if I can help it. (*Short pause*) I know many of you geriatrics out there remember me for my role as Shakuntala. You loved my histrionics . . . I loved my histrionics but . . . but . . . I don't think I was right for the part. It belonged to my sister. A very kind, beautiful, generous, evolved soul. Like Shakuntala. Something I can never be in this lifetime. But what the hell. Who wants to be generous and evolved when you have two dancing feet . . . Oops. Mine are unavailable, temporarily. But that won't keep me from dancing. (*She begins to sway and clap*) Dance away! And act like life is one big performance with a standing ovation waiting at the end of it! Spin me around! Oh this wheelchair is too small for all the life that's left in me.

Vinay leans the wheelchair on the back of its wheels and spins her around. Music.

A spot picks up the young Nazia dressed as Shakuntala, whirling like a Kathak dancer.

NAZIA. Come on, spin me up! Don't stop! Thank you! Thank you, Zarine! I will see you in Paradise!

Ruby is in a spotlight too applauding her mother.

RUBY. Proud of you, Mother! I am so proud of you!

The lights fade out on both the young and the old whirling, while Ruby continues to applaud.

THE END

The Big Fat City

A Stage Play

A Note on the Play

Usually when I read a script that comes to me for my consideration, I can figure out how it's going to play out. But with *The Big Fat City*, I had to read it twice at one go and I was still completely at sea. I found the characters fascinating, especially Lolly, the character that Mahesh wanted me to play. Here was a role that would allow me to flex my creative muscle. I immediately knew I was in for a challenge.

Having worked with Mahesh before, when

Facing page: Achint Kaur as Lolly and Nasirr Khan as Sailesh in the play. (*Courtesy Salamat Hussain*)

145

he directed me in the thriller *Double Deal*, I had complete faith in him. And, in any case, working with him would be a learning experience, since he believes in taking his actors through a rigorous workshop process, making sure there is integrity between the text, the acting and the mise en scène.

Mahesh took a while to get to the actual text. We would have fun doing the scenes in gibberish—one of Mahesh's favourite exercises to loosen up the actors' voices and remove any dependence on the actual text to convey meaning. Mahesh's plays are an actor's delight precisely because they contain so many layers. The task of unearthing these layers rests entirely with the actors. But in spite of the workshop process I somehow could not get under the skin of Lolly. She continued to elude me as a character for a very long time. The fact that she is a TV star did not help either, but I could relate to her relationship with her son. In spite of being a famous star, Lolly, in my mind, was quite a regular woman as a mother, caught up in extraordinary circumstances. (Later, Mahesh told me that the reason he cast me was that he knew I would treat her TV-star status as a regular thing and would not focus too much on indicating her star stature.)

It was only after the second show that I figured out how to play Lolly, but it was all still in my head. I was angry and went up to Mahesh to express my frustration. I felt we were all doing our own thing and not doing enough justice to the script and the characters. He called for more rehearsals, something that all of us willingly made time for.

There were some scenes where I could play her truthfully, like when she has to prioritize what she needs to do next. Of course, the character has her own bizarre set of priorities, which is what makes her so interesting and elusive at the same time.

It was only when we took the play to Bangalore—playing on a makeshift stage in a banquet hall for a very exclusive audience—that I felt I finally cracked the character. It was a revelation! I could understand her aching vulnerability, being as she is in the public eye constantly. She is blind to her own actions till the very end. I feel that there is still so much more to discover about this character—the more I perform the role, the more layers I become aware of. That is the power of Mahesh's writing. There is always a sense of the character being one step ahead of you.

While intellectually I understand the character, it will take me a long time to feel the truth of the character in her entirety. One of the fascinating devices in the play is the use of text messages to reveal what the character is really thinking or feeling. Lolly's relationship with her son is hidden from the world of the other characters, yet the audience is only too aware of what is going on in her private world through the exchange of SMSs and video clips with her son. Her son never comes on stage and yet he is an important character in the play.

Of the other characters, I can relate to Harjeet completely. Coming from the UP/Haryana belt, it is possible for me to identify with the milieu and the strong set of values that Harjeet brings with him on to the stage. These are values that may shock us in the city and yet might help us question our own ethos—something that the play, in turn, compels its audience to do.

Today, as actors of *The Big Fat City*, we have collectively realized that if we play the characters with gravity and depth, the humour is bound to spring out of it organically. That is the way it is written. It depicts ordinary people caught in extraordinarily tragic situations, each struggling to deal with their own situations in a bizarre way. It is a black comedy in the true sense of the word.

Achint Kaur
TV, film and stage actor

The Big Fat City was first performed for the public on 22 June 2013 at the Tata Theatre, NCPA, Nariman Point, Mumbai, with the following cast (in order of appearance).

MURLI	Ivan Rodrigues
NIHARIKA	Pooja Ruparel
SAILESH	Nasirr Khan
LOLLY	Achint Kaur
ANU	Sonal Joshi
KAILASH	Shashi Bhushan
PUNEET	Aadar Malik
HARJEET	Vinay Sharma

In subsequent performances the role of Harjeet was also played by Gagan Singh.

Mahesh Dattani

Cast of the video sections in the play:

NEWS ANNOUNCER   Supreet Bedi
ON FIELD REPORTER   Spatica
RAHUL   Vivaan Parashar

Director   Mahesh Dattani
Producer   Ashvin Gidwani
Photography Director   Salamat Hussain
Editor and Graphic Designer Nishantni Josson
                            and Inaayat Ali
                            Sami
Sound Recording   Ultra Video Works
Technical Director   Inaayat Ali Sami
Assistant Director   Gagan Singh
Sets and Lights   Raghav Prakash
                            Mishra
Sound Design and Music   Inaayat Ali Sami
Make-Up and Styling   Sachin Ghate and
                            Ratna Rao
Light Operations   Chetan Chand
Sound and Video Operations Nikhil Bagore

Production and Publicity Stills	Salamat Hussain
Costumes	Achint Kaur and Aayushi Kothari
Production Manager	Vijay Shukla
Stage Manager	Sudhir Sakpal
Stage Assistants	Dilawar Shaikh and Lalit Mahto

Act I Scene I

*A compact one-bedroom-hall-kitchenette.
We see it all, including the balcony of the
bedroom and also the tiny loo.*

*One section of the wall is used as a screen to
project the text messages. White projections
indicate outgoing messages. Red ones
indicate incoming messages. Each message
stays on the screen till the next one appears,
unless otherwise specified.*

*The flat is new and is missing a few
essential items such as a television set and
an air conditioner. Even the furniture seems
makeshift except in the bedroom. The*

bedroom seems to be overly cluttered with women's stuff. Bollywood-style outfits are hanging on the closet door, dumb-bells are lying around, etc.

Niharika is busy lighting up candles around the room. Murli is trying to pull down his silk kurti. He is clearly uncomfortable in it.

MURLI. Can't I wear my regular shirt, please?

NIHARIKA. Stop fidgeting with that kurti. You will tear it. No, you can't.

Murli's cell phone beeps with a message.

NIHARIKA. That must be him asking for directions. Look at your message, Murli!

Murli goes to his phone which is on a table and checks his message.

SCREEN *(from Sailesh)*: WHICH FLOOR?

MURLI. He is asking which floor?

NIHARIKA. Well tell him, for goodness' sake!

Murli texts him.

NIHARIKA *(going to the kitchenette)*. And make sure he is in the right block!

SCREEN *(from Murli)*: FOURTEENTH FLOOR.

MURLI. I've sent the message . . .

NIHARIKA *(going to him)*. Please, Murli, don't look so helpless . . . You have to look more confident! Please!

MURLI. I would feel a lot more confident if I wasn't wearing this blouse.

NIHARIKA. Kurti. You have to look successful. Now keep that unbuttoned and show a bit of your . . . Oh my God! You are wearing that banyaan. He is coming up now and I want you to get out of that banyaan now! Quickly!

Niharika begins to pull him out of the kurti. He resists.

Mahesh Dattani

The doorbell rings.

The kurti tears.

NIHARIKA. It's torn! (*Most upset*) One chance! We have this one chance and you want to ruin it?

Murli calms down for a second before he goes back into his befuddled state.

MURLI. What do I do now?

The doorbell rings again.

NIHARIKA. Hurry and change. He is your friend, remember? And you are very happy to see him.

Niharika pushes Murli to the loo and runs to the door and opens it.

NIHARIKA (*sticking her head out and calling*). Sailesh! Come back! Hi! Come on in!

During Niharika and Sailesh's interaction, we see Murli trying out shirts from a portable zip-up wardrobe in the loo.

Sailesh, conservatively dressed in a business shirt and black trousers, enters.

NIHARIKA. Hi! I am Niharika. You can call me Nikki!

SAILESH (*not sure whether to shake hands or not*). Hi Nikki. I am Sailesh Ganatra.

NIHARIKA. Come on in. (*Calling*) Murli! Your friend is here.

SAILESH. Nice flat.

NIHARIKA. Thanks! Of course we still haven't done it up. So, it's a bit bare . . . right now.

SAILESH (*looking around*). One BHK?

Niharika deftly guides him to the settee.

NIHARIKA. Do sit down. Yes it's a one BHK but we plan to buy out our neighbour. We bought this because of the location. Close to where the action is (*laughing at her own joke*). One of his colleagues lives in Vashi. Heaven knows how they can have a life there.

SAILESH. I live in Vashi.

NIHARIKA (*without losing a beat*). What will you have to drink? (*Before he can answer*) Let me get you some orange juice.

Sailesh gets a message.

Mahesh Dattani

SCREEN (from Meena Ganatra): HE
CALLED ON THE LANDLINE. ANY LUCK?

*Niharika moves to the kitchen to pour out
some juice for Sailesh. But pops into the
loo first.*

*Sailesh in the meantime is sending a text
message.*

Murli opens the door a crack.

MURLI (*whispering*). Can I wear one of my office
shirts?

NIHARIKA. You look like a bloody clerk in them!

SCREEN (from Sailesh): JUST GOT HERE.
HIS WIFE IS A PRETENTIOUS, SNOOTY BITCH.
CHANCES ARE SLIM . . .

NIHARIKA. Just—wear whatever you want and
come out!

*Niharika traipses off into the kitchen
humming to herself. Murli takes out a beige
shirt and wears it unbuttoned.*

*Murli comes out a changed man, his open
shirt revealing a smooth chest.*

MURLI. Sailesh! Old buddy!

SAILESH. Murli! Hey look at you.

They hug.

SAILESH (*laughing*). Look at you, yaar.

Murli poses trying to look self-assured.

Niharika steps in with the juice.

NIHARIKA. I am so glad to see two college mates
united thanks to Facebook.

Niharika notices his unbuttoned shirt.

NIHARIKA. Anyway, I will leave the two of you to
catch up on old times. I am going to get dinner
ready.

*Niharika goes to the kitchen and proceeds to
take out food from packages and put them
in the microwave. But her attention is clearly
on the conversation.*

MURLI (*slowly buttoning up*). Good to see you after
so many years! You look the same!

SAILESH. Yeah . . . So damn good for you, man. Associate Managing Director, Lotus Inc. India. Wow!

MURLI. You are not doing badly yourself. You own a bank, right?

SAILESH (*laughing*). Not exactly own! I am the managing partner of Jalaram Bank.

MURLI. Yes. Owned by the diamond merchants of Surat!

NIHARIKA (*popping out*). Darling, didn't we read an ad from the bank for housing loans?

SAILESH. Yes, we have only just started spreading the manure a bit!

NIHARIKA. That's when Murli told me 'Hey, guess what? That's my friend's bank. We were roomies in IIT.' Well, I say it's a pretty small world! (*Laughing in an artificial way*) Murli, you must help your friend out with some business. You know, get them to transfer their loans to Sailesh. (*To Sailesh*) Everyone we know is moving into bigger, better homes. (*To Murli*) Murli, maybe you can start with yourself.

After providing that cue Niharika goes back into the kitchen.

SAILESH. Yes, that will be good. We charge 0.5 per cent less than other banks.

MURLI. Oh good. Then maybe we can start with our loan.

SAILESH. Okay.

MURLI (*obviously hopeful*). Okay? You mean . . . you will do it?

SAILESH. I will have my loans department call you for all the documents.

MURLI. Sailesh, I need your advice. No, actually, I need your help!

Niharika steps in with some nibbles.

NIHARIKA. Oh, don't be so dramatic, Murli. It's nothing major but . . . Sailesh, we have been a little behind on our EMIs.

SAILESH. I guess that should be fine. We will calculate the EMI amount based on Murli's income and yours combined.

NIHARIKA. That's where there might be a slight issue.

SAILESH. How slight?

NIHARIKA. You see, Murli wasn't quite happy with his job. So he quit.

SAILESH. He quit? Are you mad?

MURLI. I didn't! I was fired! I lost my job!

A brief silence.

The doorbell rings.

NIHARIKA (*after looking daggers at Murli*). I think I better get that.

Niharika goes to answer the door.

Lalita Jagtiani (Lolly) enters. In her early forties. Still thinks she is a star.

NIHARIKA (*all smiles*). Oh, Lolly!

LOLLY. Nikki sweetheart!

They air-kiss on both cheeks. Lolly has two bottles of wine with her.

Sailesh stands up on seeing her.

LOLLY. I got something for your guest.

NIHARIKA (*taking the bottles*). Oh, Lollypops, you shouldn't have. Is Kailash coming?

LOLLY. He will, he will. Just making sure that Rahul's party doesn't get too—you know.

Lolly saunters into the hall.

Niharika goes into the kitchen with the bottles of wine. She quickly gets out her cell phone and taps a message.

LOLLY (*to Sailesh*). Hello. So you are Murli's long-lost friend.

SAILESH. You are Yamini!

LOLLY. Well, I was. Lalita Jagtiani.

SAILESH (*taking out his cell phone*). Oh, my wife has seen all the thousand episodes of *Saas Bani Saperan*. You were brilliant!

Murli's cell phone beeps. He checks his messages. The banter between Sailesh and Lolly continues.

SCREEN (*from Niharika*): I INVITED HER SO HE WILL BE IMPRESSED. IT'S WORKING, SO PLEASE DON'T SCREW THINGS UP. DON'T SAY A WORD.

SAILESH. So how does Murli know you?

LOLLY. Oh, didn't Nikki tell you? I live on the floor above.

NIHARIKA (*popping out*). She has the whole floor. In fact, we wanted a top-floor apartment but we couldn't because—Lolly has it all! Quite honestly, I didn't know who she was. I hardly watch television. We just started to chat and we—became such dear friends! I just thought it might be a good idea to invite her and Kailash as well. Excuse me while I get the food ready.

SAILESH. Oh, can I have some of the wine Yamini has brought?

NIHARIKA. Oh, yes! Certainly. Murli come and help me with the wine.

Murli obediently follows his wife into the kitchen.

LOLLY. You know, please call me Lolly. I am done with Yamini!

SAILESH. Oh, yes, yes. Sorry. Lollyji . . .

Lolly's cell phone beeps. Lolly has her phone

*in her hand and keeps waving it around. She
checks her message.*

SCREEN *(from Ekta)*: LOLLY I GOT 46
MISSED CALLS FROM YOU. STOP BUGGING
ME. I HAVE 6 FILMS RELEASING THIS FRIDAY.
IF I NEED YOU I WILL DEFINITELY CALL YOU.
LOVE. EKTA.

LOLLY. Oh, that is Ekta Kapoor trying really hard
to get me in her next soap. Oh, how I hate turning
down friends!

*Lolly responds to the message even as she
talks nonchalantly.*

LOLLY. Actually I am fed up with television. I am
doing something more—you know—meaningful.
Like theatre.

SAILESH. Theatre? You mean plays?

*Simultaneously Murli is trying to get the
bottle of wine opened.*

LOLLY. Yes! Not just any old play. I am very

selective. I am doing one of those serious plays by Hamesh Dattani. There is so much more depth to that kind of work.

Lolly sends her message.

SCREEN *(from Lolly):* SORRY EKTA. BUT PLEASE, PLEASE GIVE ME A RUNNING CHARACTER IN YOUR NEW SERIAL. I REALLY DON'T WANT TO DO THAT MORBID DATTANI PLAY. I AM DESPERATE. PLEASE!

The bottle pops open finally. Murli is relieved. He pours it in the appropriate glasses and brings them over to Sailesh and Lolly.
Niharika brings some more nibbles.

LOLLY. Oh, you should have chilled it a bit. Never mind . . .

The doorbell rings.
Niharika and Murli exchange glances.

SAILESH. Have you invited more people?

LOLLY. Oh, that must be Kailash—my husband. Let me get that.

Lolly goes to the door and opens it to let in a disturbed Anu. She is young and attractive, smartly dressed.

She is on the phone and walks straight into the bedroom.

ANU (*on the phone*). No! Darling, you are not listening. Sweetheart, just li . . . But he never . . . (*Inside the bedroom, more aggressive*) Just shut up! Shut your face! Fuck you! He just put his arm around me and kissed me on the cheek. All producers do that! But to hell with you! If you think I'm having an affair with him, so be it! Yes, I am sleeping around with that dodo. That's why I am struggling along, right? Ya, I'm sleeping with him. He is right here in my bedroom. Goodbye!

Anu hangs up dramatically and sits down on the bed, breathing heavily.

The others in the living room are recovering from what they've just heard.

Mahesh Dattani

LOLLY (*hesitantly pointing at Murli and then to Niharika*). And whose sister did you say she is?

NIHARIKA. Cousin. Just visiting.

LOLLY. She's been here for two months.

NIHARIKA. Well—I better see if—poor cousin Anu is all right. Excuse me.

Niharika goes into the bedroom.

LOLLY (*to Sailesh in a low tone*). You know, there is something not quite right about this whole thing.

SAILESH. I got the same feeling too!

Running parallel to this—

NIHARIKA (*to Anu in a low tone*). Why are you here? We had planned this a week ago.

ANU. I know, I know. Sorry. Did I ruin your little get-together?

NIHARIKA. I hope not!

LOLLY. You can see through it, right?

SAILESH. Yeah! The minute they said they wanted their loan transferred I knew he had been fired.

LOLLY. WHAT?

170

ANU. Anyway, I will leave. Sit in Barista for a while and you can call me when you are done.

NIHARIKA. Thanks, Anu. I really appreciate that.

LOLLY. You mean he lost his job?

SAILESH. Didn't you know? What were you talking about?

LOLLY. Oh I meant her—

ANU (*coming into the living room*). So sorry for that. Boyfriend issues. Who doesn't have them? (*To Lolly*) Lolly, you know, every time I see you in the lift I want to say something but get absolutely tongue-tied! You are an inspiration! Would it be asking for too much if I took a picture with you? For my mother and sisters. You just sit right there and I will stand behind you.

> *She gives her phone to Murli, who takes a picture when they pose.*

LOLLY. You are all right. I don't care whose sister you are.

SAILESH. Take some pics of me too!

> *Sailesh gets close to Lalita.*

Mahesh Dattani

Murli takes a few pictures from Anu's camera.

LOLLY. No, wait!

Lolly gets really cosy with Sailesh and plants a kiss on his cheek.

Murli takes a pic.

Lolly's cell phone beeps again.

LOLLY (*checking her phone*). Oh, that must be Ekta again. She can get persistent.

In the meantime Sailesh is looking at his pictures.

SCREEN (*from Rahul*): WHERE'S DAD? EVERYONE IS HERE. SEND HIM HERE OR COME AND SORT THINGS OUT YOURSELF!

Lolly is perturbed. She gets up.

SAILESH. You took them on Anu's phone! Take some on my phone. Here. (*To Lalita*) Er—do you mind? Once more?

LOLLY. I—need to see if Rahul is all right. They're

172

having a party. Taken up the entire house. Excuse me, I will be right back.

Lolly exits.

Sailesh stares at her agog.

SAILESH. She's not bad! I'm sure a lot of movie stars attend her parties.

NIHARIKA. It's her son's party.

ANU. I better get going. Have fun, guys.

The front door was left ajar when Lolly went out.

Kailash Jagtiani stumbles in and falls face down on the floor.

ANU. Wow. You really are having a party!

Niharika and Murli run to Kailash.

NIHARIKA. Kailash! Are you okay?

MURLI. He's drunk.

NIHARIKA. I'll call Lolly.

ANU (*exiting through the front door*). Well, good luck. I'm out of here.

MURLI (*trying to prop him up*). Make some coffee

for him. (*To Sailesh*) Give me a hand.

SAILESH. Shall we just take him up to his home?

MURLI. This is fairly routine around here. Lolly will come and get him. Their servant can lift him up with one hand. Last week he passed out on the terrace.

> *They manage to prop him up. Kailash mumbles something.*

SAILESH. Can you walk to the sofa?

> *Kailash mumbles something and attempts to get up but falls down.*

NIHARIKA. I can't get through to Lolly.

SAILESH. Let's put him in the bedroom.

MURLI. Good idea.

NIHARIKA. No.

SAILESH. Where will we sit if we put him on the sofa?

MURLI. Exactly.

NIHARIKA. Just put him down in a corner on the floor.

> *Niharika sends a text message.*

SAILESH. We can't do that to Yamini's husband! What will she think of us?

NIHARIKA. Okay, okay. Put him in there. I'm sure Lolly is on her way.

> SCREEN *(from Niharika)*: KAILASH IS HERE. COME WITH BANWARI AND CARRY HIM HOME.

They take Kailash to the bedroom.
Niharika gets a message.

> SCREEN *(from Lolly)*: OH NO NOT AGAIN! NIKKI DUMP HIM IN A CORNER SOMEWHERE PLEASE. RAHUL'S PARTY IS IN FULL SWING. I AM SORTING SOME THINGS OUT.

Murli and Sailesh are trying to get him on the bed when Kailash's head bobs up and then hangs limp.

SAILESH. What is it?

Mahesh Dattani

MURLI. I don't know. Is he trying to say something?

SAILESH. Yes, I think so. Listen.

Finally it's clear. Kailash pukes.

SAILESH. Oh shit! He is puking. Get out of the way.

They both let go of Kailash who falls limp on the bed after puking on his own clothes.

NIHARIKA. Oh my God! Get a towel quick!

Murli rushes to get a towel.

NIHARIKA. Anu will throw a fit. I can't bear it.

Niharika picks up a perfume bottle and sprays it.

MURLI (*returning with towel*). That's Anu's Chanel No. 5. She *will* throw a fit!

Murli begins to mop up the vomit from Kailash's pants.

SAILESH. I think we need to get him out of those.

NIHARIKA. Let it be. Lolly can do what she wants with her husband's puke!

SAILESH. We can't let Yamini's husband lie in his own puke!

176

MURLI. Any suggestions?

SAILESH. Yes! Tell Yamini to get some clean clothes for him.

Sailesh begins to undo Kailash's trousers.

SAILESH. Help me, yaar!

Murli begins to help him.

Niharika looks on helplessly.

NIHARIKA. This isn't quite turning out the way I thought it would! I am sorry, Sailesh. We just wanted to socialize a bit and then maybe talk shop a little bit.

SAILESH. Don't worry. Let's see if I can sort out your mess.

MURLI. This isn't our mess, it's Lolly's.

SAILESH. I meant your loan stuff.

They have now stripped Kailash of his pants and shirt.

NIHARIKA. Oh my God. That stinks!

MURLI. We should never have bought this flat! What's wrong with Vashi?

NIHARIKA. I am talking about the stink from his clothes. Go put them in the washing machine and do a quick wash.

Murli takes the clothes holding them at arm's length.

SAILESH. Get his wallet out first.

NIHARIKA. He has no wallet. She doesn't give him any money. The drunken fool would be dead if he had money to buy booze!

SAILESH. Still—a man has to have a wallet, yaar. Even just for pretence.

MURLI. I do that! I even keep my cancelled credit cards in my—

NIHARIKA. Go put those wretched clothes in the damn machine!

Murli proceeds to the loo where the washing machine is, puts the clothes in and starts the washing.

Sailesh looks at Kailash sprawled on the bed in his underwear and socks.

SAILESH. Never imagined someone like Yamini

178

would have a husband like that.

NIHARIKA. What did you expect? Brad Pitt?

SAILESH. Well, yeah! Someone like Brad Pitt would be perfect for Yamini.

NIHARIKA. Come on, let's get on with our evening.

Niharika goes to the living room. Sailesh follows.

NIHARIKA. Would you care for some nibbles? There is cheese and pineapple and—

SAILESH. No, let's get to the point. How bad is it?

Niharika takes in a deep breath.

NIHARIKA. The recovery agents are calling us. We were behind by six months. Then we started paying up but that was just the interest and penalties . . .

SAILESH. I know how these banks work. What happened? I mean, with his job?

Murli has come back in.

MURLI. I put it on high-spin. Will wash away all the puke. Sailesh, they fired me.

SAILESH. Why? I know you. You are super smart when it comes to computers and things.

MURLI. You don't know. Lotus Inc. US is going down under. The US mother company did not get a bailout package because it outsources to us. So if they shut down their offices in Mumbai, Bangalore, Hyderabad, they would get some money from their government. (*Upset*) What's going to happen? I will never get another job like that! What do we do? I even asked my mother if we can go live with her in Thirunalvelli.

NIHARIKA. How can you even think I will live with your mother in that godforsaken place?

MURLI. I can't take it! I can't live in the fear that those thugs from the bank are going to come and knock on our door! They will beat us up! Break some bones to get us going. I don't like violence! I don't even play Angry Birds!

The doorbell rings.

Murli jumps like a scared rabbit.

MURLI. They are here! Sailesh, help us! Please, for old times' sake!

NIHARIKA. Just shut up! It's Lolly I'm sure.

Niharika opens the door.

Anu enters with Puneet close behind her.

ANU. I am so sorry, Nikki, but I need to get this guy to clear all his stuff— (*Turning to Puneet*) What are you waiting for? Just take your stuff and get out!

PUNEET. I am sorry, sweetheart.

ANU. I am not your sweetheart any more. Just— It's over Puneet. Take your stuff and get out.

PUNEET. You mean you don't love me any more?

ANU. I want to focus on my career, Puneet. Now don't get so emotional. It will hurt for a while and then you will get over it. (*Sitting down*) Look, I am tired now and we are disturbing these people. I am not in a mood to argue with you. Just go to my room and take your things. Please.

PUNEET. You won't talk to me?

ANU. All right. Tomorrow. Not now. (*To Niharika*) Sorry, yaar. I need a drink.

Sailesh offers her his glass of wine.

Puneet slowly goes into the bedroom, with a heavy heart.

Mahesh Dattani

>*In the bedroom Puneet notices the semi-naked Kailash sprawled on the bed.*

>*Puneet lets out a moan and hits a table.*

ANU. I knew it. He will start crying now. Let him be.

>*Puneet lets out an angry cry and pounces on Kailash.*

>*Kailash lets out a frightened cry.*

ANU. Started. Men, I tell you!

>*Puneet begins to strangle him. Both of them screaming.*

ANU. So bloody predictable!

>*The screaming gets worse, with Kailash thrashing his legs about and maybe knocking down something.*

ANU. A bit more emotional than usual I must say. Where's my drink?

>*The screaming now turns to a whimper.*

MURLI. Do you want to go in and see if they are all right?

ANU. He will be fine, don't worry. His temper just

comes and goes. What do you mean 'they'?

NIHARIKA. Oh, nothing. You see, Kailash, Lolly's husband, was drunk so we put him in there.

Kailash now has turned limp. Puneet is breathing heavily but still on top of Kailash.

ANU (*getting up, sensing trouble*). Oh no! Oh fucking no!

Anu runs into the bedroom.

ANU. Puneet! No! Leave him alone!

Anu tries to get Puneet off Kailash.

The others come in.

Puneet rises.

PUNEET. You are mine! No one can take you way from me.

ANU. But, but . . . I don't even know him.

PUNEET. Sleeping with strange men will not give you love! I will give you love!

Niharika and Murli are trying to revive Kailash in the meantime.

Mahesh Dattani

NIHARIKA. He is dead.

ANU (*to Puneet*). You—did this for me? You killed
a man for me?

PUNEET. Yes, sweetheart.

ANU. Oh, sweetheart!

Anu and Puneet embrace.

Niharika's phone beeps.

SCREEN (*from Lolly*): WILL BE THERE IN
5 MINS! YOU GUYS ARE SO SWEET. MWAAAH!

*Murli backs away. His cell phone begins to
ring. He looks at the number and answers.*

MURLI (*into phone*). Ammaaa! (*Breaking down*)
Ayyo, Amaaaaaaa!

FADE TO BLACK.

Act I Scene II

A few moments later. As the lights come on Murli is babbling on the phone to his mother in Tamil.

Anu is sitting on the bed. Puneet is sitting on the floor, his head resting on Anu's lap, weeping. Anu caresses his head as if he were a child.

MURLI (*in Tamil*). Amma, why is it that this has to happen to me? I don't want this job, I don't want this city! I just want to come home and . . .

Niharika snatches the phone from Murli.

NIHARIKA (*on the phone*). Hello, Amma. How are you? . . . (*Listening to Murli's mother*) Nothing.

Mahesh Dattani

His urticaria is acting up. When his rash gets too itchy he starts bawling . . . Don't worry . . . (*Gently slapping Murli for Amma's benefit*) Stop scratching yourself. Don't worry, Amma. I am there, no> I will take care of him. You must excuse me now. There is something on the stove. Bye . . .

> *Niharika casually goes into the kitchen and quickly pulls out a large kitchen knife. She darts into the bedroom brandishing the knife.*

NIHARIKA (*pointing the knife at Puneet*). Get that murderer out of my home!

> *Anu is taken aback. She starts to guide Puneet out of the bedroom.*

> *Murli's cell phone beeps. He looks at his message.*

> SCREEN (*from Amma—it's written in Tamil and a translation is below for the benefit of those who don't read Tamil*):

186

WHEN THAT RAKSHASI IS NOT AROUND, YOU
CALL ME AND TELL ME WHAT HAPPENED.

ANU. Now wait. Nikki, just put that down.

PUNEET. It's okay, sweetheart. Darling, will you
wait for me?

ANU. Where are you going?

PUNEET. To jail! I will call the police right away.
(*To the group*) Let the world know I did it for love!

ANU. No! Don't call anyone.

NIHARIKA. I will call the cops. He killed a man in
my flat!

SAILESH. Yamini's husband! How can you take
away someone's love and say you did it for love?

ANU. Oh, bullshit. Lolly couldn't care less. But I
do care. (*To Puneet*) I am going to get you out of
this, okay? . . . Okay, baby?

Puneet nods, whimpering.

ANU. Good. Just shut your mouth for now and we
will be fine. (*To Niharika*) Look, Nikki, you know
I am here in your flat for a reason. You needed the

187

extra money and I needed a place to stay. Nobody wants to rent out a place to a single woman in this city. And we kept it our little secret, right? We told society we are sisters, right? We helped each other out. So now . . . I do want you to sort out your problems. I can help you.

NIHARIKA. How?

ANU. We still help each other out. I give you some more money and . . . what happened just now . . . you tell Lolly exactly what I tell you to.

NIHARIKA. And become an accomplice to murder? No way! Oh no! Never!

ANU. How much do you owe the bank?

Niharika pauses, putting the hand with the knife down.

NIHARIKA. You mean? All of it?

MURLI. No, Nikki, don't! She will ask us to cut the body into pieces put them in our car and dump them in the mangroves!

ANU. We don't have to hide the body. You won't have to do anything. All you have to do is sit here.

NIHARIKA. And the body?

ANU. Leave that to me. You just have to sit there. Puneet and I will do the rest.

NIHARIKA. Eighty lakh. Plus another five in penalties and interests for non-payments.

ANU. Eighty-five.

Murli scratches himself on the arm.

MURLI. My urticaria is really acting up!

ANU (*going to Murli*). You do want it to stop for good, don't you?

SAILESH. Don't forget, I saw what you did.

MURLI. Yes! Sailesh! Thank God. Make some sense of all this. You tell me what to do! Pal, remember I always shared my murukkus with you in the hostel. For old times' sake, please! What the hell do we do?

SAILESH. Relax. Let me handle this.

Sailesh goes to Anu slowly in an intimidating fashion.

SAILESH. I am a Gujarati. We don't like to get involved . . . One crore.

189

Murli begins scratching his chest.

MURLI. My ointment! I need my ointment!

ANU. Twenty-five.

SAILESH. Out of the question. Lolly will be here any minute.

ANU. Precisely. Your darling Lolly with whom you are having an affair and whose husband you strangled in a moment of possessive rage.

SAILESH. What nonsense!

ANU. I have some cutesy pictures to prove it. And I can hire some really good lawyers . . . And you don't want inquiries into your finances or your personal life because whatever it is you are hiding—and everyone is hiding something or the other—will be all over *Mumbai Mirror*. Now be a good Gujju and don't get involved.

Sailesh is uncomfortable.

SAILESH. Make it forty, please!

ANU. Forty! Interesting figure. Why?

SAILESH (*blurting it out*). I need it! I made some . . . adjustments . . . in my client's bank account and I need to put that money back before I'm found out.

ANU. Hmm. Okay. Puneet sweetheart, come with me.

Anu and Puneet go into the bedroom. The others follow.

Anu notices for the first time that Kailash doesn't have clothes on.

ANU. He is almost naked!

PUNEET. Sweetheart, where did you put his clothes?

ANU. I didn't! Oh, you sweet boy! You think I and he were . . . Oh! I love you, baby.

PUNEET. I love you too, baby!

ANU (*as if to a baby*). Really. How much? Show me?

PUNEET (*showing with his hands*). Such much.

ANU. Such much?

PUNEET. Sachi muchi such much.

NIHARIKA. Are you serious? You guys are unreal.

ANU (*suddenly turning to Niharika*). I have never had anything more real happen to me in my life! . . . We don't have much time! Where are his clothes?

We hear the washing machine going into spin mode.

MURLI. Er—they are almost done. Spin-dry.

ANU. Never mind. If he is drunk, he can be naked also. Grab his head.

Puneet and Anu lift Kailash's body.

MURLI. What are you doing?

ANU. Stand near the balcony.

MURLI. But what—

ANU. Just shut up and stand there!

Murli goes to the balcony.

ANU. Look out.

Murli is frozen.

ANU. Look out! . . . And tell me if anybody is out on their balcony.

Murli looks around.

MURLI. No, there is nobody.

ANU. Look up. Left. Right. Down.

Murli follows her directions.

MURLI. No . . .

ANU. Then step aside.

Anu and Puneet carry Kailash's body to the balcony.

ANU (*swinging the body*). A one—a two—and, THREE!

They toss the body over the edge.

Pause. The washing machine makes a loud noise as it goes into its final spin.

A police siren is heard.

SAILESH. That was quick.

Murli violently begins to scratch his back. He tears his shirt off and flings himself on to the sofa groaning in agony.

Fade out on washing machine as it shudders into a high-speed spin.

FADE TO BLACK. END OF ACT I.

Act II Scene I

A few minutes later.

Niharika is applying ointment on Murli's chest which is now red with a rash.

MURLI. I will never wax my chest. I will never wax my chest.

Anu is on the phone.

ANU (*in Haryanvi*). Hahn, Bhaiya. I want to make the picture with them. They are decent people, not haraamis like those other fellows . . . Okay . . . (*Listening*) Okay, Bhaiya! Thank you, Bhaiya! . . . Yes, yes, it's a mind-blowing script. That part was written for me.

MURLI. What script?

SAILESH. The one we are getting paid for.

ANU. Hahn, Bhaiya. Okay . . .

Anu hangs up.

ANU. All going well. My brother will transfer the money into your accounts tonight. Which means it will show in your accounts on Monday. So I've kept my end of the bargain. Congratulations, Murli, the flat is all yours. Congratulations, Sailesh, your ass is covered.

MURLI. What script were you talking about?

ANU. The one you guys have written. I had to tell my brother something. I can't say, 'Bhaiya, my boyfriend murdered someone so now I need to pay off the witnesses.'

NIHARIKA. So what exactly did you tell him?

ANU. Look, he knows I am here in Mumbai to get into movies. He is willing to finance a film if there is a good role in it for me. So . . . you and Sailesh are the directors of the film.

MURLI. What?! I mean, what do we have to do now?

NIHARIKA. Now don't get so worked up, your rash is getting worse.

MURLI. But, but. When her brother finds out we are not—he will kill us!

SAILESH. Yes! I told you I don't like getting involved!

ANU. Relax, guys. You won't get involved. Have the police come knocking on our door? No. They all assumed he jumped off the terrace. Right? That's the pattern in this city, right? One woman jumps off with her kids, another one jumps off with her boyfriend, a man jumps off with his boyfriend and now this one jumped too—without his clothes . . .

They all stare at the washing machine.

ANU. Give them to Lolly when you see her tomorrow. Tell her he took them off before leaving. Poor thing, she must be at the police station or somewhere . . .

MURLI. But your brother . . . Won't he come and kill us all when he finds out there is no movie?

ANU. Not after I tell him what my Puneet did for me.

SAILESH. You mean, you will tell him what happened?

ANU. Yes.

NIHARIKA. The truth?

ANU. Yes.

NIHARIKA. Which is?

ANU. That horrible man tried to molest me. He promised me that he would get me a role through his wife's contacts.

And then, and then he forced himself on me. Fortunately, my saviour, my love, came and saved me from a life of dishonour. He killed the man in a moment of passion. Then my dear, dear friends Nikki, Murli and Sailesh came up with this master plan to toss his body out of the window and pass it off as suicide. Out of gratitude I promised them freedom from their woes. What is a crore plus if it cannot buy you back your honour?

MURLI. What if he doesn't like Puneet?

ANU. Puneet and I will get married next week. So he will definitely like Puneet.

MURLI. So—you are sure—we won't get into trouble?

ANU. Think of a good script just in case.

MURLI. Just in case what?

ANU. No. You won't need to, so relax.

NIHARIKA. So, what next?

ANU. Sailesh will say goodnight and leave. Downstairs there will be quite a commotion with the watchmen talking about what happened. Crowds gathered around the spot where he fell. A cop posted there. Sailesh will ask out of curiosity what the matter is. The watchmen will tell him that TV star Lalita Memsaab's Saab committed suicide. Sailesh will exclaim in horror, 'Oh my God! My friends don't know about this!' You will then call us and break the news gently to us. We will all come down horrified and ask the watchmen all the details. 'Poor, poor Lolly!' We will go cluck-cluck. 'Poor, poor Rahul!' Cluck-cluck. And we will all agree with the other residents: 'Such a thing shouldn't happen in a decent society like ours!' Tchee, tchee. 'We hear he had a drinking problem.'

Oh, how sad! 'His wife drove him to it.' Oooooh!

NIHARIKA. Lolly is a dear, dear friend of mine and I would never agree to a remark like that!

ANU. Good. You're getting the hang of it.

NIHARIKA. No, I mean it.

ANU. Oh, come on! It's all nonsense. As if you care about Lolly.

NIHARIKA. How would you know, anyway?

ANU. I do! I have lived in this city long enough to see beyond that crap, so don't give me that 'I care about Lolly' nonsense.

Pause.

SAILESH (*to Anu*). So, I go down. I ask. I come back.

ANU. No, you call.

SAILESH. I call. Right. And . . . the money will be transferred, right?

ANU. It will be in your account on Monday.

SAILESH. No hanky-panky?

ANU. No.

Mahesh Dattani

SAILESH. Because if I don't get it, I am going to call the cops, tell them the truth. That this guy threatened to kill us too if we said anything, and so on.

ANU. Goodnight.

SAILESH. Goodnight.

Sailesh stops at the door and looks at Puneet.

He goes to Puneet.

SAILESH. You know, if I came home and found a naked man in our bedroom, I would kill my wife.

PUNEET. You don't love her?

SAILESH. Of course I do. That's why I would kill her.

PUNEET (*to Anu*). What does he mean?

ANU. It means . . . He's just waiting for an excuse to kill his wife.

Sailesh thinks about it.

SAILESH. Hmmm. Interesting thought.

Sailesh exits.

The others look at each other.

NIHARIKA (*sarcastic*). What next, Captain?

ANU. We wait for his call. Then we all go down. Do our clucks and then Puneet will kiss me goodbye and go home.

PUNEET. Darling, I want to spend the night with you! I know you need me!

Puneet tries to hold her in his arms.

ANU. Not now, darling, not now. Later.

There is a commotion outside. Men yelling 'Chalo, chalo, ek line mein . . .'

Some girls screaming.

Murli peeps out. He comes right back in.

NIHARIKA. What is it?

MURLI. Remember the cops who came so soon after we . . . Well, they are here to raid Lolly's son's party.

NIHARIKA. What on earth is there to raid in Rahul's party?

The door bursts open. Sailesh brings in a troubled Lolly, covering her face with a veil.

LOLLY. Oh! Thank God for neighbours like you!

Lolly hurtles towards Niharika, sobbing violently.

LOLLY. Oh, Nikki! Why? Why me?

NIHARIKA (*comforting her*). There, there, my sweet Lollypops. It must be awful, I know.

ANU (*quickly*). Nikki. We don't really know what's bothering her, do we?

NIHARIKA. Yes! I mean no! Now, Lolly, sit down. Let me get you some wine and you tell us what this is all about.

LOLLY (*grabbing Niharika's arm*). You mean, you don't know?

NIHARIKA, ANU, MURLI, PUNEET (*all in unison*). No!

LOLLY. How do I begin to tell you?

All wait for her to break the news.

LOLLY. Kailash's clothes are gone!

They all look at each other.

MURLI (*stealing a quick look at the washing machine*). Oh dear.

ANU. You mean, the dhobi did not return them? That's sad.

LOLLY. No!

NIHARIKA. And . . . where do you think they are?

SAILESH. And . . . why are these clothes so important?

LOLLY. That's exactly what I mean—How do I begin to tell you?

Lolly's cell phone beeps. She looks at her message.

SCREEN (from Rahul): MOM! WHERE THE FUCK ARE YOU? THEY ARE TAKING US SOMEWHERE TO DO TESTS ON US. I GAVE THE COP MY WATCH TO LET ME KEEP MY CELL PHONE. COME AND GET US OUT OF THIS HELL! PLEASE!

Lolly lets out a deep groan.

LOLLY. Where do I begin? OH! I am a bad mother! Bad, bad, bad! (*Not letting go of Niharika*) How

Mahesh Dattani

could I do this to my own son? I let them take him away while I am hiding . . . and I got him into this mess. He is a clean boy. It was my idea! Oh! What am I to do! A poor, lonely woman with a son in jail because his mother . . . ! Oh my God! What am I saying? (*Looking at their blank faces*) I am not making any sense, am I?

They shake their heads.

NIHARIKA. Maybe if you tell us a little more about what happened? Calmly? Take a few deep breaths. Come on, Lolly.

Lolly takes a few deep breaths.

Her phone beeps again. She looks at her message.

SCREEN (*Anonymous*): EITHER GIVE US BACK THE PACKET OR THE MONEY.

Lolly takes in a few more deep breaths.

Her phone beeps again. She looks at her message.

SCREEN *(from Rahul)*: MOM!!! IF YOU
DON'T GET US OUT I WILL TELL THEM
EVERYTHING!

Lolly starts hyperventilating.

LOLLY. Where's that wine you promised?

*Niharika offers her Sailesh's glass which he
left untouched.*

Lolly drinks the wine in one large gulp.

LOLLY *(with renewed strength)*. Okay. Where are
Kailash's clothes?

ANU. Where's Kailash?

LOLLY. He is dead.

*Everyone gets into the attitudes of shock
and surprise as rehearsed.*

NIHARIKA. Oh my God! How?

ANU. What? Dead? How?

MURLI. Oh, Amma!

PUNEET. Kailash dead? Who killed him?

LOLLY. All of you are such phoneys. You all know.

Lolly goes to Puneet.

LOLLY (*pointing a finger at him*). You killed him!

Silence.

Puneet is nervous. He looks at Anu.

PUNEET. I don't know what you mean.

ANU. Yes. Please explain.

LOLLY (*to Puneet*). Never mind how I know. Just give it to me. Just give it to me!

ANU. Lolly, can you please explain clearly what is it that he has to give you?

LOLLY. You don't fool me! He knows exactly what I'm talking about.

ANU. Trust me. He doesn't.

SAILESH. Neither do we.

LOLLY. He was spying on me!

ANU. And why would he do that?

LOLLY. Ask him. Were you not hiding behind my car this morning?

Puneet looks sheepish.

LOLLY. There. See! See! He has nothing to say.

ANU. Puneet, were you hiding behind her car?

PUNEET. Yes. But I was not spying on her.

LOLLY. Yes, you were. You saw me hand over the packet to Kailash!

PUNEET. I saw that. But I was not—

ANU. Puneet, what the fuck were you doing hiding behind her car if you were not spying on her?

PUNEET (*after some discomfort*). I was spying on you.

ANU. On me? Whatever for?

PUNEET. I—I thought you didn't love me any more! I was waiting for you to come out of the building . . . I thought you were in love with some other man!

ANU (*melting*). Awwwww!

LOLLY. Enough. Both of you are a team, I know. Give me the packet now.

PUNEET. What packet?

LOLLY. The one you killed my husband for!

PUNEET. I didn't kill your husband—for the packet.

ANU (*quickly*). He didn't see anything. Certainly not the packet.

SAILESH (*also trying to save the situation*). That's right. (*Going to Lolly*) Lolly, you are having a hard night, I know. First, the tragic news of your husband, then the raid where your son is being tested for drugs, and a missing packet that clearly you value above all else.

Lolly leans on his shoulder.

LOLLY. Oh, at last, someone who understands. Oh, Sailesh! It's not easy being a woman.

Lolly puts her arms around him. Sailesh pats her.

SAILESH. There, there, let it all out. I am there for you.

LOLLY. Oh, Sailesh!

SAILESH. Lolly!

LOLLY. Saileeeeesh!

Lolly first gets a little amorous and then uncontrollably so. She kisses him hard on the mouth.

SAILESH. No, Lolly! (*After the kiss, his eyes popping out, grinning*) Golly!

LOLLY. That should tide me over this night. (*Patting Sailesh's cheek*) Later. (*Turning to Puneet and Anu, a determined woman*) He knew everything! He saw what happened in the car. When Kailash took off his pants to hide the packet in the secret pocket, this man was pressing his nose against the window. Tell me, if he was spying on you, why was his nose pressed against my car window?

PUNEET. I thought—they were doing something in the car. You know . . .

ANU. You pervert!

LOLLY. He saw him put the packet in the secret pocket. And I know you killed him. So there is no point lying any more.

PUNEET (*more with a sense of wonderment*). How do you know I killed him?

ANU. Why do you think he killed your husband?

LOLLY. He knew how much the packet was worth. Fifty lakh at least in a party. So you killed him, stripped him naked and threw his body over the balcony. Thinking people will assume he jumped off the terrace like all those women. Well, I know he didn't jump off the terrace. I was on the terrace hiding from the cops. I knew about the raid!

NIHARIKA. Er—Lolly. His pants are in the washing machine. The packet is still in there.

LOLLY (*relieved*). Oh, thank God!

NIHARIKA. Problem solved. Murli, go get the clothes.

> *Murli goes to the bathroom.*
>
> *Lolly is overjoyed.*

LOLLY. Oh, Nikki! I knew you would be lucky for me. I suppose after this pervert killed my husband and stripped him naked, you grabbed his clothes and saved their precious contents for me. It just doesn't make sense but I don't care as long as I have— (*Seeing Murli with the clothes*) Oh!

> *Lolly rushes to Murli and grabs the wet trousers. She turns the legs of the trousers inside out and slips her hand inside a pocket that's sewn in. She takes out a wet polythene bag with nothing in it.*

LOLLY. It's gone!

MURLI. I put it on high-spin, so . . . it must have torn the packet and . . . washed it all away . . .

Lolly looks at the bag and then at Murli. She lunges at him.

LOLLY. You washed away fifty lakh of—

Sailesh and Niharika try to hold her back but she has enough strength to knock them down. Murli screams.

Finally, Lolly lets out a cry of anguish and sinks to the floor.

Sailesh goes to Lolly again.

Murli screams again but with rage.

Niharika goes to Murli and tries to calm him down.

MURLI. Why me? What did I do? Why did I lose my job? Why didn't some other fucker lose his? One thing. One thing I thought I did right, put that dead fucker's clothes for a wash and that also is all wrong. It's my fault! I should have guessed he had drugs stuffed in his pants! Aaaargh!

I can't take this itching any more!

Murli scratches himself violently.

NIHARIKA. Stop it, Murli. Don't!

Niharika manages to grab hold of Murli's hands and prevents him from scratching further.

LOLLY. I am dead. What am I to do?

SAILESH. Relax, Lolly. I am here for you . . . First things first. Aren't you going to get Rahul and his friends out of jail?

LOLLY. You don't understand, Sailesh. I have to give them the money or they will do horrible things . . . like throw acid on my face!

SAILESH. No, I won't let them!

LOLLY. I can't even step out of this flat now—you saw that *Mumbai Mirror* photographer in front of my door! I can't go home, Sailesh. I can't go home because the cops, the drug mafia and the media are all after me! Do you understand? I now have to rely on the kindness of Nikki to hide me here.

MURLI (*pleading to Niharika*). Let's go! Let's pack

our bags and leave right now! I will call my mother and tell her we are coming!

SAILESH (*consoling Lolly*). Not to worry. Things will be all right.

LOLLY. And—and I don't have twenty lakh on me.

ANU. You buy the stuff at twenty and retail it for fifty. Good work!

LOLLY. One has to live! This is what happens to us when Ekta stops taking our calls!

SAILESH. I will sort it out. I will get you the money.

LOLLY. Really? How?

Sailesh looks at Anu.

SAILESH. I have my resources right here.

ANU. No.

SAILESH. The budget for the film just went up by twenty lakh.

LOLLY. What film? Is there a part in it for me?

SAILESH. Yes, of course! (*To Anu*) Call your brother and tell him we have signed on Yamini to play your mother.

LOLLY. I am not ready to play mother yet. But what the hell. These are desperate times.

Anu is hesitant.

SAILESH. Oh, come on. That's the least you can do for her. Considering . . .

ANU. I am not sure it will work.

SAILESH. You have no choice.

ANU. Oh yes, I do. What will you say to them? I am going to tell them the truth—You killed him because of your affair with Lolly.

LOLLY. What? You killed my husband?

SAILESH. No, Lolly. It's a bit more complicated than that.

LOLLY. More complicated than what? Either you killed him or you didn't.

PUNEET. I killed your husband. I found him sleeping with my girlfriend!

LOLLY. WHAT? Are you mad?! Kailash hasn't slept with anything except the bottle in the last ten years. (*Suddenly patting Sailesh*) Oh, darling. I am so happy I found you . . . Later, later.

ANU (*to Puneet*). Sweetie, I wasn't sleeping with him.

PUNEET. Darling, you always think I am stupid. But I am not that stupid. He was lying naked on your bed. Give me one good reason why he would do that if he was not sleeping with you.

MURLI. There is a simple explanation. You see, he was drunk, he passed out. But before passing out completely, he puked. So Sailesh and I took off his clothes and put them in the machine. Then Anu came and then you came and then she told you to go in there and get all your stuff and leave.

PUNEET (*growling, going to Murli*). You expect me to believe all that cock and bull? You think I am stupid, huh?

MURLI. Why did I bother explaining? (*To Puneet*) Er—no. Sorry, I was only trying to help.

LOLLY. So . . . when will I get the money?

ANU. Monday. I will call my brother tonight and tell him to send another twenty. It will come in Murli's account. He can make out a DD.

LOLLY. Am not sure the underworld will accept a DD.

ANU. Just put the money in your account and draw cash.

Lalita is overjoyed.

LOLLY. Oh, thank you! Oh my! What a relief! At least I won't have the underworld on my back. Now what's next? Oh yes, my son! My son! Poor Rahul. I am a terrible mother!

SAILESH. Lolly, let's go together now and get your son out of the lock-up!

LOLLY. Oh, will you help, Sailesh? Oh, I can already see you as a father to Rahul!

SAILESH (*carried away by the role*). Yes! Let's go! And get—our son!

NIHARIKA. And he doesn't even know yet that there's a slight change of papa for him.

LOLLY. The cops want a lakh to get all the kids out. They are all in there except the movie stars' kids. Faiz Khan came personally and got his son out. A lakh is the going rate for each kid.

SAILESH. A lakh is nothing for our son.

Sailesh looks at Anu.

ANU. I don't have a lakh on me!

LOLLY. Murderers! You made me a widow!

ANU. I can draw 40,000 from my ATM. Do you think the price is negotiable?

LOLLY. No. They are very correct about these things.

SAILESH. I can draw 20,000.

NIHARIKA. How much have we got?

MURLI. 2000.

SAILESH. That's only 62,000. Damn!

LOLLY. I think Banwari will have 40,000. That's what he makes on tips at my parties. He's saving it to send to his gaon.

SAILESH. Perfect. So let's all get our ATM cards, find Banwari and go get my son!

They all scramble to get their bags.

SAILESH. I am only thirty-four and I have a seventeen-year-old son!

Mahesh Dattani

LOLLY. Oh, Sailesh! When I saw Kailash's body on the street—I knew he had left to make way for better things! I am so happy I don't need to feel guilty about anything!

SAILESH. Neither do I! My wife can now openly carry on with our neighbour. She will be so happy when I tell her!

NIHARIKA. Let's go.

They all gather around at the door.

Sailesh opens the door grandly.

A sudden series of flashes as photographers have a field day taking Lolly's picture. Her screams are drowned in the photographer's questions and 'Ma'am, look this way', 'Ma'am', 'Ma'am, smile', 'Ma'am'.

FADE TO BLACK.

Act II Scene II

A news format similar to NDTV 24×7.

NEWS ANNOUNCER. Coming up next: the stock market plunges to an all-time low as more and more multinational companies pull out of the country after the President of the United States, Bobby Jindal, withdrew tax benefits to US companies who made losses on their Indian operations. But before that let us look at our special report on the Yamini story!

> *A clip from her TV serial plays. A 'Madras cut' of her close-up.*

NEWS ANNOUNCER. Popular television actress of the '90s, Lalita Jagtiani, best remembered for her role as Yamini in *Saas Bani Saperan*—

*Visual changes to the one where the four of
them are caught off-guard coming out of
Niharika's apartment.*

NEWS ANNOUNCER. —who was unavailable for
comment on Saturday after a drug bust on the
party of her teenage son was discovered by our
camera person Naresh, hiding in a neighbour's flat.

*We see an excerpt of that spot interview.
Lolly is trying to avoid the camera. Sailesh
is pushing aside journalists. Anu and Puneet
are in the background.*

SAILESH. Please, please. Have some consideration.
She has just lost her husband.

JOURNALIST. But is it true that he committed suicide
to avoid being caught having drugs?

SAILESH. Please! This is all nonsense. Have some
respect! Where are the drugs? Have they found
any drugs? All completely baseless.

*Change of visual to the exterior of the building.
A reporter waits patiently for her cue.*

NEWS ANNOUNCER. Now we have an update on

that story from Swati Rangarajan who is at Lalita's building where it all happened last Saturday. Swati, can you tell us what exactly do the drug test reports of the party revellers show?

SWATI. Thanks, Varsha. I have just heard from the ACP office that the drug test results show that they were absolutely clean. Yes, Varsha, the lab technicians unofficially confirmed that. Also, Varsha, it is interesting to note that there were no drugs found on the premises so the police are now closing the case. We have just received information that Lalita's son has been released and no charges have been filed.

NEWS ANNOUNCER. Well, thanks, Varsha, for that update. Now on to—

SWATI (*interrupting her*). Varsha, I see them driving into the building.

The visual shows Swati scrambling towards Lalita's car, the cameraman too is running with the camera.

Lolly steps out wearing really large shades, her head covered demurely in a white

> *dupatta. She constantly dabs the edge of her*
> *shades with a white handkerchief to suggest*
> *she has been crying.*
>
> *Her son, Rahul, gets out of the car too,*
> *wearing a white T-shirt to suggest mourning.*
>
> *Sailesh steps out as well, holding Lolly's*
> *arm. He too is wearing a white kurta and*
> *dark glasses.*

SWATI. Lalita, you must be devastated—

LOLLY (*interrupting her*). I just want to thank all my fans who tweeted me all those messages of support.

SWATI. The drug tests showed that—

LOLLY. It is their support that keeps me going. I know exactly who is spreading all these rumours. The extent to which people go to get a role. But I shall not name the actress. I lost my husband. They framed my son. Now I fear for the safety of my son.

SWATI. Can you tell me why the police thought that your son—

LOLLY. Oh no, no. I am not going to name her.

> *Her phone rings. She moves away from*

the camera but the camera keeps her in the frame while Swati interviews Rahul. Sailesh follows Lolly and he listens, as Lolly gets tense over the conversation.

SWATI. Rahul, have you ever tried drugs before?

RAHUL. What do you mean before? I run an anti-tobacco club in college! I am a Greenpeace activist! And I am a vegan. What the [*bleep*] do you mean by before? Before what? [*Bleep*]! I am innocent! Can someone please believe me? Stop this shooting! Go away, all of you! Nobody cares! My life is ruined because nobody cares to know the truth—

Lolly, in the meantime, is torn between her conversation and seeing her son all worked up. She and Sailesh run to Rahul who is almost knocking down the cameraman. Swati is trying to extricate herself from the wires that are tightening around her neck in the melee. Sailesh covers the camera with his hand . . .

BLACKOUT.

Act II Scene III

Day. Soon after the interview with Lolly.

Lolly and Sailesh storm into Niharika's flat. They are wearing the same white clothes and shades that they wore for the TV interview.

LOLLY. Where's that woman? Where is she? Anu!

Lolly stomps into the bedroom. Anu is seated on the bed, her usual spark missing.

LOLLY (*screaming at her*). Where's the money? You promised it will reach his account by Monday. It's Tuesday! Those thugs are coming to get me!

ANU. You will get it!

Anu goes to the living room. Lolly and Sailesh follow.

SAILESH. When? If I don't put that money back in the bank I'm screwed. You promised!

NIHARIKA. Er—Sailesh . . .

LOLLY. Nikki, do something. I lost a husband, you lost my drugs, the whole world thinks my son is a druggie—why am I the one losing everything? Nobody else seems to have lost much.

MURLI. Lolly, you have to help us!

LOLLY. Now what? I am not doing anything more unless I get the money upfront! What do you want me to do?

MURLI. Make a movie!

Harjeet comes out of the bathroom wiping his hands with his handkerchief and then rolling down his sleeves.

ANU. Lolly, I would like you to meet my brother— who is funding our film project.

Harjeet is too taken away with meeting 'Yamini' the TV star.

225

Lolly goes to Harjeet and delicately offers her hand.

LOLLY. Hello, Sirji! I am Lalita Jagtiani.

Harjeet takes her hand and doesn't let go of it.

HARJEET. Hello. Hello. What a pleasure meeting you at last. My mother wants me to take a photograph with you . . . Anu, take a picture.

Harjeet poses with Lalita while Anu takes a picture with her cell phone.

Harjeet puts his hand on her waist for another picture. Sailesh coughs.

SAILESH. I will take some more pictures later . . . Sirji. Er—maybe we need to talk business.

Harjeet suddenly turns serious.

HARJEET. Hmmm. Business. Yes. (*Sitting on the sofa, spreading himself so nobody can sit next to him*) Okay. Why so much hurry to talk business?

Lolly's cell phone rings.

LOLLY (*into the phone*). Not now! I'm in the middle of something important.

Lolly hangs up.

SAILESH. Well, you see, we had many discussions with your sister . . . based on which we were assured certain advances . . . based on which we made certain other commitments . . . so now those other—commitments have to be met . . . so it will be nice if you could er—part with the money you promised us.

Lolly's phone beeps with a new message.

Lolly reads her message.

SCREEN *(from Rahul)*: MOM, WHY THE FUCK AREN'T YOU ANSWERING? THERE IS A GOONDA IN OUR HOUSE! HE'S LOCKED ME IN!

Lolly is unsettled again.

LOLLY. Look, I need to go. I need to check on something.

Lolly hurries to the door.

HARJEET. Wait . . . please.

LOLLY. Look—I'll be back.

HARJEET. Stay a while. Convince me about the—business. And I will transfer the money into your accounts from Anu's laptop.

Lolly stops. Another beep. She looks at her phone message.

SCREEN *(from Rahul):* HE IS GOING TO BREAK MY ARM IF YOU DON'T COME.

Lolly is unsure.

LOLLY. Five minutes.

HARJEET. What's the hurry?

LOLLY. My son is calling me.

HARJEET. Mamma's boy. Can't do without his mother. I used to be like that. Remember, Anu?

ANU. Yes, Bhaiya. Mummy was also fond of you. It was always about you.

LOLLY. Er—this is somewhat of an emergency, so . . . if you don't mind . . . Can we . . . get on with it?

HARJEET. Oh, I am sorry. If it is really an emergency, please go. I don't want to keep you from your son.

LOLLY. No, no, it's okay.

HARJEET. I thought it was an emergency.

LOLLY. Not yet.

HARJEET. Good . . . I really like your acting.

LOLLY. Thank you.

HARJEET. Show me a scene.

LOLLY. Huh?

HARJEET. Act out one scene for me, please.

LOLLY. I—I can't.

HARJEET. *Ek chota sa scene. Mere liye. Paise laga raha hun bhai.*

LOLLY. Okay. Okay . . . Let me—give me a moment. (*Striking a pose as if she's about to begin, then dropping it*) I can't! I haven't rehearsed the scene.

HARJEET. Who wrote the scene?

    Silence.

    Harjeet goes to Anu.

HARJEET. I thought you said the script was ready.

ANU. It is, Bhaiya. (*Pointing at Murli*) He wrote the scene.

Murli starts to scratch his bottom.

Harjeet goes to Murli.

HARJEET. So explain one scene to her and let her enact it. Okay?

Murli nods.

HARJEET. So start.

Harjeet makes himself comfortable on the sofa again.

Lolly looks at Murli.

MURLI. Actually, Sir, he is the writer.

Murli points at Sailesh.

HARJEET. I don't care who has written it. I want to see a scene. So show me.

Sailesh steps forward.

SAILESH. Certainly, Sir. Let us do the er—climax scene. Well, you see the character has had some unfortunate dealing with the drug king Usmanbhai . . . Lolly has to return the money—

HARJEET. Lolly?

SAILESH. Lalita, I mean the character Lalitaji will play.

HARJEET. Useless name. Change it. Hmmm. Go on.

SAILESH. And now the drug king has sent his goon to threaten her. She goes to her friend—she is desperately in need of money—but the goon is at her friend's home, threatening her friend.

Sailesh gestures to Lolly to begin.

Lolly pretends to come in. She acts it out to an imaginary figure in the room and also to Niharika.

LOLLY (*running to Niharika*). Oh, Nikki! Something terrible has happened! It's so—terrible, I can't tell you about it. I must have some money or my life is in danger. (*Noticing the man*) Aaaah! He is here. What are you doing? Stop right there! You will not harm my friend! Whatever you wish to do, you can do it to me! But leave her alone! She is innocent! Have mercy! Mercy!

Her phone beeps.

SCREEN (*from Rahul*): MOM! HE BROKE MY LITTLE FINGER! IF YOU DON'T COME WITH THE MONEY HE WILL BREAK MY WRIST!

Lolly begins to cry—for real this time.

LOLLY. I can't! This is all real! Usmanbhai has sent his goon to my place. He just broke my son's little finger! Aaargh! God, help me! Please! Please have mercy and give me the money! (*Grabbing Anu's laptop which is on the table*) Here. (*Putting it in front of Harjeet*) Please! Transfer the money or they will break my son's arm and throw acid on my face. Do it now! I beg of you!

HARJEET. Very good! Really good!

LOLLY. No! It's all too real! It's very real! Please, someone help me! (*To Anu*) Your boyfriend murdered my husband!

ANU (*startled into the scene*). Lolly, no!

LOLLY. Help me save my son!

HARJEET. Mind-blowing scene!

LOLLY. This is not a scene!

SAILESH (*holding her*). Calm down! (*To Harjeet*) These method actors. They want to make it as real as possible.

Lolly fumbles with her phone. She shows

Sailesh the message.

Sailesh is shocked. He steps forward, weighing his words.

SAILESH. Er—Sirji. There is just one small pressing issue. You see when your sister told Lalitaji that she would receive an advance of twenty lakh, Lalitaji made a commitment to somebody else. So she—we—need that money—like—right now . . .

Pause.

Puneet enters.

ANU. Puneet! I told you to stay away!

Harjeet glares at him. Puneet is stunned to find Harjeet there.

PUNEET. Harjeet Bhaiya . . .

HARJEET. *Scene toh ab shuru hone wala hai.* (*To Anu*) Our father sent me here. To find out what's going on . . . You sounded pretty scared when I told you . . . about his new position over the phone . . .

Lolly's cell phone beeps. She looks at it. It is an MMS.

The screen shows a traumatized Rahul.

233

He is in a moving taxi, a sling around his neck for his arm.

RAHUL (*on screen*). He left soon after breaking my arm. He will be back tomorrow for the money. I won't be there . . . Why, Mom? What did I do to deserve this? What had Dad done to you that you killed him? You are not a bad mom . . . no. You are a bad person. By the time you get this, I will be gone. Bye, Mom.

Lolly falls limply on the sofa. She gives her phone to Sailesh.

ANU. I just wanted a life!

LOLLY. I just wanted him to have a good life!

HARJEET. And us? Why did you want to ruin things for us? What about our lives?

LOLLY (*to Niharika*). Where did he think the money for his college, his trips to Europe with his friends, donations to Greenpeace came from—I paid for all that!

HARJEET. You think I don't know? Huh? You think I don't know what is going on? On the Saturday-night news we see that Lalita Jagtiani's husband has committed suicide by jumping from the terrace of his building Deja View. Even as Dadaji remarked, 'Isn't that the same building our Bhateri is in?' you called about your film project. Half an hour later you call again to say Lalita Jagtiani is acting in your film! *Arre wah!* The night she loses her husband she signs another project that too with you. Only one thing can make a person so shameless. Greed.

LOLLY. Greed . . .

HARJEET. Yes, I will keep my hard-earned money. Why should I give it to any of you?

SAILESH. No! You can't do that! You will give us the money when you hear what happened.

ANU. Sailesh, no! Trust me, let me handle it!

SAILESH. Hah! Fat chance he is going to give us any money unless we tell him why we deserve it.

ANU. You fool! It's a trap.

SAILESH. What have we got to lose? (*To Harjeet*) Your sister and her boyfriend killed this poor woman's husband. She was trying to cover up for that by bribing all of us.

HARJEET. Ah, I see! Why?

SAILESH. Why? Because they are getting married, that's why!

PUNEET. Yes! We have applied—

Harjeet slowly takes out a gun and checks whether it is loaded. He puts it back in his hip pocket.

Harjeet looks at all of them. After a while . . .

HARJEET. Let me tell you a story. If you like it I will give you the money to make it. Okay?

Niharika and Sailesh nod their heads in agreement.

HARJEET. What about you, Lalitaji? Would you like to listen to the story? There is a role in it for you too. Without a stupid name like Lolly. Don't worry—you still get to play a mother.

LOLLY. A mother? And you think I will play it well?

HARJEET. Yes. You are a mother, aren't you?

LOLLY. I am . . . an actor. I know how mothers must act.

HARJEET. Good. This story won't work without you.

SAILESH. She will do it.

HARJEET. Good . . . There are too many stories set in Mumbai. I don't like that. The true stories are from other places. The story should be set in a town. In Haryana. In Rewari.

PUNEET. Rewari?

HARJEET (*looking at him*). You know where it is?

PUNEET. Yeah . . . I—

Harjeet looks at Anu and Puneet. After a while.

HARJEET. The story has . . . Dada, Dadi, Maa, Pitaji and four children . . .

ANU. The youngest daughter is called Bhateri, which means 'Enough'.

HARJEET. That is not the story.

ANU. That is part of the story. The youngest was a curse. A girl again. Enough! No more!

HARJEET. Maybe. Maybe towards the end . . .

ANU. And the beginning.

HARJEET. No. The beginning is about the brother and sisters. So shut up!

ANU (*quietly*). Yes, Bhaiya.

HARJEET. The brother has a passion. He wants to make movies. Not any arty-farty type but real movies. He is only twelve but he gets his sisters together and with his 16mm camera he makes movies with his sisters. What was that scene where you got an applause from Dadi?

ANU. Bhaiya would tell me to cry. And I would start immediately (*imitating the 'crying child' from a '60s movie. Short gasps and clenched fist over eye*). And then he would shoot, yelling, 'Don't stop crying till I tell you to stop!' (*Enacting the scene like a child actor*) Oh, Bhagwan! Please take my life! But save my brother's life. Without my brother my mother won't be able to live. So why do you want to take two lives? Instead, please take my life! Oh God! Please listen to me! Take my life instead of my brother's. Please!

Harjeet applauds.

HARJEET. See? That's a scene! That's a story! Sacrifice! Do you people know what sacrifice means? Huh? Do you? No? We want a good story or not? Huh?

Harjeet looks at Sailesh. Sailesh nods.

SAILESH. Yes. We do!

HARJEET (*to Anu*). Then understand what sacrifice means! . . . The children grow up. All are married. First the brother—to a nice girl from the neighbouring village. The two older sisters—to nice boys from far-off towns . . . And then it's Bhateri's turn . . . But by then Bhateri wanted to act. So she comes to her brother and begs him to convince their father and grandfather about letting her act in TV serials. After all, the entire family watches *Saas Bani Saperan*. The brother thinks, 'I didn't get a chance to join movies, at least let Bhateri fulfil her dream.' Sacrifice. Get it? So the brother convinces their parents to let her go, and she is off to Mumbai . . . Hmmm. All stories, no matter where you start them, end up in Mumbai.

But wait . . . That is not the real story, is it?

Harjeet looks at Anu and Puneet.

HARJEET. Is it? What we didn't know was she had a special playmate. None of us knew about him. Clever girl. Not even I. She tricked us into thinking she was off to Mumbai to do TV serials. The real reason was she wanted to elope, without anyone missing her. She fooled us. After all, our Bhateri is smart. Everything is fine. She gets small parts to convince us that she is working on being a TV star. She even chose to stay here as a paying guest to live near our favourite TV star, Yamini. All is well until her playmate kills Yamini the TV star's husband. And this is what we see in the news.

Harjeet takes out his cell phone and shows a YouTube clip.

SCREEN: *A grainy news clip without the voice. The scene when they are caught unawares by the camera. We see Anu and Puneet in the background.*

HARJEET (*while showing the clip around*). First Dadi remarks, 'Isn't that our Bhateri?' And then Mausi exclaims loudly, 'Wait! Isn't that our Mange Ram's son, Puneet? What is he doing in Mumbai? I thought he was in England. Could it be? That he and Bhateri?' . . . (*Going to Anu and Puneet*) All hell breaks loose. Dadi cries and bangs her head on the wall. Mummy stays silent. And to think that just a couple of days before Father has become the head of the panchayat. The khap panchayat.

MURLI. Khap! That's what she keeps mumbling in her sleep!

HARJEET. Ah, so you knew what was coming. You knew that sooner or later you two will be found out. You planned to run away. Where? Wherever you go, the khap will find you.

Harjeet pulls out the gun and aims it at Puneet and Anu.

Niharika screams.

HARJEET. That's how the story needs to end. Sacrifice. The honour of the village is more important. My sweet little Bhateri and her sister-fucking lover. It's my sacrifice.

Puneet embraces Anu in a protective way.

HARJEET. See. Everybody wants to sacrifice. So be it.

> *Harjeet shoots Puneet. Puneet slumps in Anu's arms. She puts him down. She walks up to Harjeet.*
>
> *Anu spits on Harjeet.*
>
> *Harjeet shoots her. She falls down.*
>
> *The others are stunned into silence.*
>
> *Harjeet looks around.*
>
> *Harjeet begins to cry.*

HARJEET. End of story. For me. Sacrifice.

FADE-OUT.

Act II Scene IV

The stage is empty. Niharika comes out of the bedroom wheeling a large suitcase. There are other suitcases near the door. Murli comes in through the front door and takes out some.

Niharika stops and looks around the flat.

Murli joins her.

MURLI. You will like Thirunalvelli.

NIHARIKA (*looking at him*). I will?

MURLI. Our balcony is as big as this flat.

Niharika looks around.

NIHARIKA. Still. This was ours.

MURLI (*nodding*). This was ours. (*Putting an arm around Niharika*) I'm going to apply to Infosys in Bangalore. I am confident . . . In the meantime . . . you should like Thirunalvelli.

NIHARIKA. You know, we tried our best to keep this. We lied, we abetted a murder . . . You know, I could do that again if I can have this flat. It's home. I can understand even killing for a home. But honour? Why would anyone kill for honour? I mean . . . what is it?

MURLI. Come.

As they turn around, Lalita enters.

LOLLY. Oh, thank God you haven't left.

NIHARIKA. Lolly! I thought you'd . . .

LOLLY. Yes, I've moved in with Sailesh. Usmanbhai gave me a good price for the flat so I bought his wife and the guy she loves—they make an adorable couple—a nice flat in Karjat. I just came to complete the society paperwork, and—I thought I'd give you a present . . .

Lalita hands them a package.

NIHARIKA. Oh, that's sweet of you. What is it?

LOLLY. Open it.

Murli takes off the wrapping. It is a painting.

LOLLY. It's a painting of Mumbai. I saw it outside Jehangir Gallery and thought the artist managed to get the feel of the city with all those people, and the old buildings! So many people just going about as if life was all about . . . getting somewhere.

Niharika hugs Lalita.

NIHARIKA. Thank you, Lolly. Thank you! We will hang it on our wall in Thirunalvelli.

LOLLY. I'd better rush. Usmanbhai doesn't like to be kept waiting.

They bid each other goodbye.

LOLLY (*at the door*). I hope you come back.

Niharika looks at the painting.

MURLI. We will. We will come back!

SLOW FADE-OUT.

Mahesh Dattani

The screen shows the painting of a Mumbai bazaar with loads of people. The credits roll on the screen as in a movie.

THE END